WICKED LADY

Tim McGirk was born in Colombia in 1952. An American, he earned a degree in journalism at the University of California at Berkeley before travelling to North Africa where he covered the Western Sahara war for UPI. He then reported on Iran, Turkey and the Gulf for a Middle Eastern affairs magazine before joining the *Sunday Times* in London, first as foreign manager, then as a features writer and member of the investigative Insight team. He co-authored *Rainbow Warrior* on the French Government's attempts to sink Greenpeace. He is married with two sons and currently works as the *Independent*'s Madrid correspondent.

Praise for WICKED LADY:

'McGirk writes in a refreshingly matter-of-fact style. There are some excellently funny moments.'
Auberon Waugh, *Independent*

'McGirk's tautly written, compelling biography – 161 pages of gazing, hypnotised, into a snakepit.'
Hampstead & Highgate Express

'McGirk's account of their lives together throws a great deal of light on the sources of Dalí's creative genius, and it's a riveting read into the bargain.'
Yorkshire Evening Post

Wicked Lady

Salvador Dalí's Muse

Tim McGirk

HEADLINE

ISBN 0 7472 3377 2

Printed and bound in Great Britain by
Collins, Glasgow

HEADLINE BOOK PUBLISHING PLC
Headline House
79 Great Titchfield Street
London W1P 7FN

Rouge the demoness
And she pales.
She lives to forget.

Paul Eluard

To Jan

Contents

Acknowledgements

I should like to thank those people who had the rare experience of knowing Gala, as well as anyone could, and who were willing to share their impressions so openly: Nanita Kalachnikov, Enrique Sabater, Reynolds and Eleanor Morse, Rafael Santos Torroella and Eduardo Fornes. I am also grateful to Liz Nash, who tracked down Gala's sister in Vienna; the staff of the Salvador Dalí Foundation in Florida; and Alan Schwarz in California for his persistent sleuthing. This work would never have been possible without Richard Cohen's patience and sound advice. And, if it weren't for Cal McCrystal and David Blundy, who encouraged the London *Sunday Times* to send me on a Salvador Dalí assignment in 1984, I would never have become intrigued by Gala.

Preface

Salvador Dalí was hideously burned in an electric fire on 4 August 1984, and the newspaper I was working for flew me out for the death watch. I concealed my ignorance from my editor; I thought Dalí was already dead – and, in a sense, he had died. Hunting down the story in Cadaqués, on the Costa Brava, where he had painted, and in Pubol castle to which he had retired, I realised that Dalí had given up living long before. His renunciation had occurred two years previously, with the death of Gala, the Russian woman with whom he had shared his life for over half a century.

I, of course, knew none of this when I began my vigil outside Dalí's hospital. However, there was one astonishing diagnosis that had come from the doctors attending him. The burns would heal, but a worse problem had arisen. Despite his millions, his many hirelings and sycophants, his friends and his nurses residing in Pubol castle, the painter had been slowly dying of malnutrition.

The uproar was huge. Were his guardians trying to profit by starving him to death? Dalí was Spain's greatest living artist, the last surviving surrealist. He was also a friend of King Juan Carlos. Inevitably an investigation was opened, and the portrait of Dalí which emerged from the many witnesses on parade was shocking, pathetic. It all had to do with Gala.

When she died, Dalí's reaction was to shut himself up in her room, draw the curtains and turn away all food. He had loved her; that was undeniable. Yet it was fear rather than love that drove him into the shuttered darkness. He was dying of malnutrition because he believed he would choke to death if he swallowed food. This phobia had seized Dalí before, but Gala had always been there to calm him. She had been his wife, his mother, his mistress, his protector and his muse. It was as if Dalí had taken refuge in her bedroom, surrounded by her Russian icons, to hide from death, as a frightened boy might cower in his mother's closet.

I began to wonder what kind of a woman could have inspired Dalí so intensely. Dalí was an awful coward, yet she had succeeded in holding his terror at bay. I thought she was a kind of saint, for I recalled that Dalí had once painted her as a madonna, floating beatifically above a small fishing harbour. My opinion of Gala altered the next day, after I met an ex-associate of the Dalís.

When this former associate greeted me at his villa, I thought he was a madman, trying to out-Dalí Dalí. My opinion changed in the course of our conversation, as this dapper gentleman pirouetted agilely away from the topic of forged Dalí prints. The Spanish press had claimed that friends and associates of Dalí's possessed 30,000 blank sheets of paper with Dalí's signature on each and that they had amassed a fortune, some say £7 million, through sales commissions while connected with the Dalís. This ex-associate claimed that it was perfectly legitimate for the artist to sign the blank papers and that he had done so at the request of Gala. I asked him about Gala. 'She liked young boys,' he said, 'and she spent a lot of money on them.' This was not what I had expected to hear about Dalí's revered madonna. Then he told me his reasons for leaving the artist's circle. 'One day, Gala said she had found someone younger and better-looking than I was. She told me to clear off.'

A few other fragments about Gala came out. I learned that Pubol castle was her escape from the Dalí circus. There she could retreat with her young lovers – and continued her sexual adventures well into her eighties. Dalí was not allowed to enter the castle unannounced; he had to await a formal, written invitation from his wife. A Catalan forger hired by Gala told me how she had attempted to seduce him and then, when he refused her advances, how she tried to force him to drink an entire bathtub full of champagne. If someone annoyed her, she would burn his flesh with a cigarette.

Some said that Gala's greed had cheapened Dalí's art, that she forced him into mass-producing careless and derivative works for a quick profit so that her taste for sex and gambling could be satisfied. Others argued the reverse: that, without Gala's pushing, Dalí would have lapsed into lunacy; without her demonic temper, the vulnerable artist would have fallen prey to exploiters far worse than his wife. Whatever else, Gala was a fanatical believer in Dalí's genius.

I grew convinced that Gala was the key to understanding Dalí. It is true that Dalí opened himself wide on canvas, exposing his fear of women, his obsession with his overbearing father and his terror of so many things. Yet, somehow, all his exhibitionism seemed totally cerebral. His own descriptions of the relationship with Gala are equally deceptive. In his autobiographies he writes of her in frank, almost pornographic, detail, but he manages to avoid exposing the core of her character.

When Dalí was moved out of the intensive-care unit several days later, I returned to London. My news article was finished, but Gala, the muse and harridan, continued to obsess me. In libraries I studied every print I could find of Dalí's Gala. He did not always flatter her. In fact, she seemed to inspire Dalí with terror as well as devotion. The newspaper archives yielded little on Gala. She was described over and over as 'Russian', as though that were a synonym for secretive, mystical and ruthless.

There was also the historical dimension that intrigued me. Gala had survived many of the political and cultural convulsions of the twentieth century. She and Eluard married in the midst of the Great War. They became leaders of the surrealist movement in Paris during the 1920s. With Dalí, Gala was swept up in the murderous anarchy in Catalonia that foreshadowed the Spanish Civil War. They fled France just as the Nazis were invading. They settled in Spain while Dalí rediscovered Catholicism and became the token painter of the Franco dictatorship. Then, in a complete somersault, she and Dalí became cultural gurus for the hippies.

Naturally enough, I decided to start my investigations on Gala with Dalí himself. All doors to the tower in Figueras where he convalesced were closed to me. Gala, I soon learned, was a taboo subject. He refused to talk about his wife and forbade anyone to mention her name in his presence. Perhaps her death reminded him of the proximity of his own. Nor were his guardians cooperative; it was in their interests to eradicate all evidence of Gala except Dalí's many portraits of her. Gala's excesses had been too sordid; they stained *el Maestro's* reputation and that was bad for business.

I also located Gala's daughter by her first husband, the French poet Paul Eluard. Cécile found it too painful to talk about her mother, for Gala had been a monster to her.

I went through stages of hating Gala. She was, I thought, a woman of genuine evil. She was cruel and greedy and vicious. Her amorality repelled me. Yet there is also much to admire about her. She had an undeniable gift for inspiring a great number of artists. Her powers worked on many others aside from Dalí. Eluard, Max Ernst, Giorgio de Chirico all fell under her sway. The surrealists had a saying that if someone produced good work he must have been 'in love with Gala'. One of Dalí's American friends explained it a bit more crudely: 'She was the first groupie.'

Sex was a driving impulse in Gala's character, and to ignore this would be to leave her portrait half-finished. Gala used sex to dominate both Eluard and Dalí, creative but weak-willed men. Sex was also a levy to be collected from the dealers and businessmen seeking to enrich themselves from Dalí's art. Making love to Gala was often a dealer's only way of getting a contract from Dalí.

This is, at times, an uncomfortably intrusive biography; it has to be. There is a strong and very peculiar sexual element to Dalí's art. André Breton, the surrealist theoretician, pointed out Dalí's 'narcissistic fixation (anal-sadistic in character)' and his compulsion to over-eroticise all objects. Obsessive themes of masturbation, sodomy and sexual dread are all so personal that it would have been impossible to write about Gala and Dalí without peering into the dark corners of their relationship. How did Gala weave herself into Dalí's strange fantasies? That is what I sought to answer.

The occupation of muse is devalued these days. Some would argue that a woman should strive for creative fulfilment on her own, not through her lover. But this criticism cannot apply to Gala; she never entertained hopes of being an artist herself. Having recognised that she had little talent in that direction, she instead channelled her energies into those writers and painters who did. For Eluard, her judgement on his poems mattered far more than that of André Breton, leader of the surrealist group. Dalí, on finishing a canvas, would nervously subject it to Gala's scrutiny. Her critiques were often harsh, but for Dalí and others there was no denying her aesthetic intuition. Through her seances, her tarot card readings and her oracular utterings, Gala played this role of muse, riding the dark currents of the subconscious with convincing verve.

If a psychological portrait were made of every great artist who had a muse, there would be one constant: the muse helps guide the artist across new thresholds by having greater conviction in the artist's powers than he does himself. This was true with Gala, but she took it to a terrible extreme with Dalí. Her power was so absolute she was able to convince him that without her he would be destroyed.

Theirs was no ordinary love affair. Even from their first meeting on the Costa Brava in 1929, it was clear that, although Gala had the gift of helping Dalí interpret and give shape to his fantastical creative impulses, he had allied himself to a dark angel.

1

Eyes That Pierce Walls

Gala lived with Salvador Dalí for fifty-three years, first as his mistress, later as his wife. She was Russian. He painted her obsessively, in a hundred different guises, and signed his best canvases with her name entwined around his. He exalted her as a kind of virgin mother, yet she possessed a monstrous appetite for money and sex. She inspired Dalí's art – and corrupted it.

They met in August 1929. She was married at the time to Paul Eluard, the poet and a leader of the surrealist movement which was scandalising the Parisian art and café society. The Eluards had a daughter, Cécile, aged eleven. As it happened, Gala was not even with her husband when a vague arrangement was made for them to visit the Spanish artist in his home at Cadaqués, a fishing village south of the French border in Catalonia.

Dalí had introduced himself to Eluard at the Bal Tabarin night-club in Paris, where the poet was spending the evening with a woman friend. Gala was in Arosa, Switzerland. Eluard had heard of Dalí in connection with a film he had made with another Spaniard, Luis Buñuel. This was a surrealist concoction in which a rotting donkey was stuffed inside a grand piano. It was news to Eluard that Dalí could also paint, and when the Spaniard offered to show him his work the poet was intrigued.

Eluard, Gala and Cécile set off by car on Gala's return from Arosa, where she had stayed for several weeks. Her absence had been too long. They had a 'liberal' marriage; both he and she interpreted this to allow lovers. They were candid about this, and Eluard took pleasure in hearing – and witnessing – her sexual adventures. Clearly Eluard had more in mind than showing his wife Dalí's paintings. Gala later said: 'Eluard kept telling me about his handsome Dalí. I felt he was almost pushing me into

1

his arms before I even saw him.' In his wallet Eluard carried a photograph of Gala nude which he would proudly show to his friends.

The reason for Gala's stay in an Alpine sanatorium was ostensibly to cure her lung ailments, but she would often dally in the Alps for several weeks with a new companion. She and Eluard had fallen in love as teenagers in a Swiss health sanatorium, and forever afterwards the Alps exerted an erotic magnetism over her. It seemed as though she was re-creating the pattern of her first, innocent courtship with Eluard. Gala had also survived several close battles with tuberculosis and pleurisy, and each check-out from the sanatorium convinced her that she must live as intensely as possible, for her life might not last long.

Eluard had his affairs too. There was a pretty girl, Madame Apfel, conveniently married to a rich homosexual, whom Eluard had pursued to Berlin. He did ask gallantly for Gala's permission first. 'I'd very much like to go to Berlin for three days. But that is, of course, if it isn't an inconvenience or doesn't bore you too much.' Gala, in Eluard's words, 'sweetly counselled' him to go.

Their courteous infidelities, however, did inflict pain on each other. A glimmer of desperation lies behind his boasting when he writes: 'My Gala, I've been making love often, too often. But what I wouldn't give to spend a night with you. Everything.' They had spent months apart, and it seems that Eluard had wanted the Cadaqués holiday to be a cease-fire, a time of wary reunion. If he was pushing Gala towards the young Spanish painter, Eluard never intended it to be more than a short affair, one in which he could share, as matchmaker and voyeur. The possibility that she would leave him for Dalí never occurred to him.

Eluard was even in the process of buying an apartment for them in Paris, one big enough for their daughter to live there with them instead of being constantly farmed out to Eluard's mother. Gala had resented the daughter's drag on her own independence.

The dirt road up the coastal mountains to Cadaqués was dangerous, and Eluard drove badly. A side-effect of the medicine Eluard took for his tuberculosis made his hands shake. The heat and dust suffocated; cicadas shrieked; and Gala was in a vile mood. The journey from Paris had lasted several days, and

Cécile, who had inherited the sickly health of her parents, was a poor traveller.

Far below them, the flat Ampurdan plain was evaporating into a wheaty haze. The villages were distant brushstrokes of white. The road had toiled up past the vineyards, the groves of olive and oak trees, and now the Eluards were driving along a mountain's sharp, slate-backed ridge. Even in summer, the high wind on the summit slapped their car. On either side were bigger mountains, purple and black, plunging into the sea. Cadaqués was only a few miles away. It was a harsh place. The villagers had lived from the sea and vineyards until all the grapes died from a strange disease, leaving only the sea to sustain them. During the centuries the men of Cadaqués had built up terraces of stone, narrow as steps, to dizzying heights on the mountain. Now and then there was a gaunt oak, exhausted and bent, like a farmer rooted to his stony plot of dead vines. The barrenness of the Cadaqués landscape, for some, is as debilitating as the heat.

All Eluard had wanted was a cheap holiday. André Breton had gone to Brittany. Some of the other surrealists had decamped to Switzerland, but since Gala had just returned from Arosa they wanted a new destination. The village of Cadaqués appeared through a cleft in the mountains. Gala saw a big church that jutted into the sea like the prow of a bright fishing boat. The church seemed to be pursuing a black, shark-fin-shaped rock in the bay. The address given the Eluards was the Hotel Miramar. It was Cadaqués's only hotel and easy to find, a white stucco building on a stone beach. The rooms were primitive, with no running water or electricity, which did not help Gala's mood. She liked a splash of cold water in the mornings. After checking in at the hotel, the Eluard family set out to find Dalí.

If their Spanish host proved insufferable, the Eluards at least had other friends from Paris staying in Cadaqués to distract them. The summer home of the Dalí family was pointed out to them, on the far point of a crescent bay outside the village. It was a whitewashed house with a eucalyptus tree and red geraniums, standing alone on a beach of black slate. The Eluards drove along as far as the rough track would take them. There on the beach with Dalí were some friends from Paris: René Magritte, his wife Georgette, and another Belgian couple, Camille Goëmans and his wife. They were all in their bathing costumes, and Dalí was

3

laughing hysterically. The others seemed embarrassed, and relieved by the distraction of the Eluards' arrival.

'If you could see what I imagine,' Dalí had been telling them, according to his autobiography, *The Secret Life of Salvador Dalí*, 'you would all laugh even more than I do.

'Imagine to yourselves, for instance, that you see in your own mind a certain very respectable person. All right. Now go on and imagine a little sculptured owl perched on his head – a rather stylised owl, except for his face which must be quite realistic. You see what I mean.

'Well, then, imagine on the owl's head a piece of my excrement!' He repeated, 'Of my own excrement!'

If Dalí had deliberately set out to make a poor impression on Gala, he could not have contrived to do so more certainly. Gala hated scatological humour almost as much as she hated dirt, and she was caked with dirt from the arduous drive. Dalí remembers Gala as irradiating bad humour and being 'rather annoyed at having come'. The Eluards made their excuses and repaired to the Hotel Miramar for a siesta. The trip must have seemed a terrible mistake.

That afternoon, Gala and Eluard gathered with the Goëmanses and the Magrittes at a terrace café, under the shade of plane trees, beside the beach. Camille Goëmans a gallery owner, had signed up Dalí to do some paintings for a November exhibition. The Goëmanses had journeyed to Cadaqués to see if Dalí could meet his promise. It seemed doubtful. Gala and Eluard found Goëmans in some despair.

As Goëmans explained it, Dalí – who later said: 'The only difference between me and a madman is that I am not mad' – had become fixated on one painting, or rather on a tiny corner of one painting. He was spending hours painting a pair of excrement-stained underpants, lavishing on it more and more detail. An earnest discussion ensued as to whether the besmirched breeches were surrealist in their shock value or merely infantile.

Their debate was interrupted by the sight of Dalí, resplendent in a silk shirt and his sister's borrowed pearls, tripping along the curved beach. The villagers of Cadaqués had come to expect such bizarre dress from Dalí, the son of a prosperous notary, but Gala and the other assembled surrealists were astonished. Dalí seemed to be challenging them, obliging them by his eccentric behaviour to proclaim his genius. Gala, for one, was unimpressed. She

4

dismissed Dalí as 'having a professional Argentine tango slick-ness'. Gala was perhaps not alone in her judgement. Georgette Magritte, wife of the painter, was more puritanical than surrealist. Once, in Paris, the leader of the surrealist group, André Breton, saw that Madame Magritte wore a gold cross around her neck. A fierce anti-cleric, Breton demanded that she remove the cross, and, when Madame Magritte stormed out, her husband had no choice but to follow. It is doubtful that Gala and she would have enjoyed each other's company. Georgette, by all accounts, was protective of her husband, while Gala found other women simply boring. Gala had no women friends, no confid-antes. An acquaintance, Denise Tual, recalls: 'Gala was an inter-esting woman for men. Eluard, Ernst, Picasso and Dalí were all charmed by her. But to other women she was always angry and jealous. She could turn on this terrible look. Bitchy.'

Gala listened as the Magrittes and the Goëmanses explained Dalí's extraordinary behaviour. Dalí himself was seized by uncon-trollable laughing fits as they all sat drinking Pernod, but his lunacy began to seem less calculated. Afterwards they strolled along the beach watching the fishermen load their nets into green, white and red boats that had night lanterns like the anten-nae of deep-sea fish. The boats pushed off into water as still and black as Cadaqués slate. Dalí was now calmer. Gala had struck him as having 'an intellectual face', and the two walked together. With typical lack of modesty, he recalls that Gala was 'immedi-ately surprised by the rigour which I displayed in the realm of ideas'. Gala confessed that initially she had thought Dalí obnoxious, but now she warmed to him and agreed to meet him on the beach the following morning.

Dalí says he awoke before dawn with a sense of anxious fore-boding. In front of his easel he was distracted by the morning sounds, a key turning in a lock, the bells clanging on a passing flock of sheep, the rhythmic splash of a fisherman's oars. In the beginning it wasn't just Gala that he was trying to impress but all of his visitors. He slashed his silk shirt, turned his swimming trunks inside out. A look in the mirror convinced him that wasn't enough. He bloodied his armpits and then dyed them blue. For a manly cologne, he anointed himself with fish glue and goat manure. He tucked a red geranium behind his ear and was about to join Gala and the others when an extraordinary thing happened to Dalí. He lost his nerve.

Glancing out of the window he saw Gala, sitting on the beach with her naked back towards him and facing out to sea. She was an androgynous beauty. Instantly, from that image, he realised that he was in love with her. 'How had I been able to spend the whole previous day with her without recognising her, without suspecting anything?' It dawned on him that his grotesque outfit was a kind of 'nuptial costume'. He continued in his autobiography: 'It was for her that I had smeared myself with goat dung and aspic, for her that I had torn my best silk shirt to shreds, and for her that I had bloodied my armpits! But now that she was below, I no longer dared to appear thus. I looked at myself in the mirror, and I found the whole thing lamentable.'

He washed off the stink and blood and clipped back the geranium. As the ultimate concession to Gala he even put his swimsuit on right. Dalí did, however, leave on his favourite pearl necklace.

What had attracted Dalí was not Gala's face, but her lean, boyish body and her 'delicate buttocks which the exaggerated slenderness of her waist enhanced and rendered greatly more desirable'. Eluard's description of her is more proprietorial: 'She has the shape of my hands.' Her most arresting feature was her eyes, liquid brown, big and round and with an intensity, Eluard once said, 'able to pierce walls'. She was not a classical beauty, but men found she gave off a strange sexual radiance. When Gala was an old woman, in her seventies, she would buy intercourse with young gigolos. She exerted an attraction over some of these lovers that cannot solely be explained by the expensive gifts she lavished on them.

Dalí, still reeking of the goat dung and fish glue that had resisted several scrubbings, made his appearance. However, every time he tried to speak to Gala or reply to her questions he was cursed with another bout of hysterical laughter.

'Since I was unable to talk to her,' wrote Dalí, 'I tried at least to surround her with all manner of little attentions.' Gala at first seemed curious about this hysterical madman who would run back from the house with cushions and glasses of water – only for her. Then, according to Dalí, Gala's curiosity was replaced by a flash of practicality. 'She considered me a genius – half mad but capable of great moral courage. And she wanted something – something which would be the fulfilment of her own myth.

And this thing that she wanted was something that she was beginning to think perhaps only I could give her!'

Dalí's odd behaviour with Gala was not lost on the others. It seemed that Dalí was getting worse, not better. Once Dalí had returned to his easel, Goëmans and Eluard mulled over an idea: if Dalí was so besotted by Gala perhaps she alone could help him. Even Buñuel, the film maker, who had known Dalí since university days in Madrid, could not soothe him. Buñuel had arrived in Cadaqués to coax Dalí into writing a screenplay for a new film, *L'Age d'or*. After the success of their first one, *Un Chien Andalou*, shown to a coterie of surrealists, a rich French viscount had agreed to finance the next project. Buñuel, however, was desperately short of ideas; he needed a lucid Dalí almost as much as Goëmans did. So the group delegated Gala to run a psychic rescue mission and pull Dalí out of his madness.

Why did Gala agree? Was she attracted to him or was it merely Dalí's unfettered egotism that made him think he had dazzled her with his art? Could she have been motivated by nothing more than benign curiosity? Her meeting with Dalí happened at a time when Gala's life had drifted into a pattern of comfortable aimlessness. Eluard was rich through inheritance and a creative leader of the Paris surrealists. Gala basked in Eluard's fame but did not contribute to it. At the surrealists' weekly gatherings at the Café Cyrano in Paris, Gala was always haughty and silent. She preferred artistic action to café intellectualising. Eluard's success was not dependent on Gala; nor did Eluard depend on her exclusively for sexual love. The gentility of their adultery masked the pain of inadequacy that Gala must have felt knowing that Eluard wasn't satisfied with her exclusively. As a mother, she had also been made expendable. Cécile was taken from her hands by Eluard's possessive mother, who found Gala a spoiled little Russian girl incapable of caring for her only son's child.

Gala never aspired to be a writer or artist, even in childhood. Neither, it seems, did she envy the creators. Perhaps Dalí's boast that Gala could only fulfil her 'myth' with him is close to the truth. Her creativity, her strength, lay in intuiting what missing parts an artist needed to complete himself and then providing them. With Dalí the sacrifice and energy required would be enormous. Dalí had true artistry; she had seen the paintings illuminating his cramped and grey Cadaqués studio. However, Dalí seemed to be overpowered by the nightmarish images that he conjured for the canvas. His arrogance concealed many private terrors. He gave no encouragement to show that she could reach him. A simple question from her about the weather, the fishermen or Dalí's family would bring on a spell of hysterics. The one advantage for her was Dalí's obvious devotion, but Gala had no way of knowing how permanent it would be – or how destructive it might be for them both. If nothing else, this devotion was flattering. Besides, Dalí was young, ten years younger than she, and extremely handsome.

She agreed to meet Dalí, alone, for a walk. She had one condition: that Dalí choose a time when he would be able to curb his hysterical laughter. Dalí replied that he had no control over his fits but that through his hysterics he would be listening raptly. 'The preoccupied air with which Gala received the answer that I had "no control" over these laughing fits gave me a mad urge to laugh,' he wrote in *Secret Life*. He kissed her hand and fled.

In the evening, as the swallows darted from their nests under the Hotel Miramar's white balconies, Dalí met Gala. Her daughter stayed behind with Eluard. On Cape Creus, the easternmost point of the Iberian peninsula, the eye of the lighthouse swept along, following Gala and Dalí's progress as they walked out of the village and into the terraced labyrinth of olive groves. They were both silent.

'It's about your picture, *The Lugubrious Game*,' Gala finally said.

She explained how this important work was marred by Dalí's fascination with excrement. As Dalí recounts, Gala ploughed on: 'If those "things" refer to your life, we can have nothing in common, because that sort of thing appears loathsome to me, and hostile to my own life. On the other hand, if you intend to use your pictures as a means of proselytism and propaganda – even in the service of what you may consider an inspired idea – we believe you run the risk of weakening your work considerably and reducing it to a psychopathological document.' This was the declaration with which Eluard, Goëmans and Dalí's other friends had entrusted her.

Dalí's reply – that he wielded excrement as a 'terrorising element' – made her grow thoughtful. Gala took his hand, and Dalí was seized again by wretched laughter. 'With her medium-like intuition she understood the exact meaning of my laughter,

8

so inexplicable to everyone else. She knew that my laughter was altogether different from the usual "gay" laughter. No, my laughter was not scepticism; it was fanaticism. My laughter was not frivolity; it was cataclysm, abyss and terror.'

'My little boy!' Gala assured him. 'We shall never leave each other.' Parts of this conversation, as reported by Dalí, are ludicrously improbable. Would Gala really have been so struck by pity and awe that she would instantly vow never to abandon him? How did she fathom that Dalí's hysteria was truly heroic, that of a visionary peering over the abyss, instead of the sniggering nastiness of an emotional infant? It would be easy to dismiss the entire episode were it not for the testimony of others present in Cadaqués. Buñuel and Georgette Magritte, in their recollections, refer to Dalí's spells of madness.

Gala and Dalí became inseparable. Gala's relationship with him, as Eluard and the others could not fail to notice, had ceased to be a detached errand of mercy. Eluard, rather disconsolately, distracted himself by playing with Cécile, a child who never stopped craving her mother's attentions, and by trying to iron out René Magritte's Wallonian accent. Magritte was not amused by Eluard's little joke and sulked, refusing all entreaties to paint while in Cadaqués. One evening, as Georgette and Eluard watched Gala disappear with Dalí on their habitual walk, Georgette asked:

'Aren't you worried?'

'No,' replied Eluard. 'I just hope she doesn't get hurt.'

Dalí's behaviour seemed to be worsening. In the meantime, Eluard's patience frayed. There was no sex, no piquancy, in the odd relationship developing between his wife and the Spanish artist; he did not feel any vicarious thrill watching Dalí's displays of slavish devotion to Gala. If anything, he felt jealous of their growing closeness.

Eluard decided to end the emotional game which he had promoted between the pair. He announced to Gala that it was time to return to Paris. Papers for the 'family' flat needed signing; clients were waiting to buy paintings and primitive art from his vast collection; several surrealist tracts were being printed. There was no scarcity of excuses for heading home, but Eluard was also alarmed.

When Eluard delivered his ultimatum, to his astonishment Gala chose to stay behind with Dalí. This had never happened before. Even during the height of her affairs with Max Ernst and Giorgio de Chirico, Gala had always returned to him. Eluard packed his bags and drove out of Cadaqués alone.

He had lost a wife but gained a painting; Dalí did Eluard's portrait. As he explained: 'I felt it incumbent on me to fix forever the face of the poet from whose Olympus I had stolen one of the muses.' Any trace of Gala is absent from the poet's portrait. She now belonged to Dalí.

2

The Missing Gold-digger

Dalí may have worshipped Gala, but he was also afraid of her. In that he was not alone. Most men and nearly every woman – for she detested rivals of her own sex – found her tyrannical. One poet likened her to a bullet fired over a desert. The trajectory of her desire never veered. She was cruel, fierce and small. Frail and sickly, she forced herself to take cold showers to build up her resistance. She collected fluffy, stuffed animals, but once she cooked up her live pet rabbit for lunch. When people annoyed her, she would spit at them. As Gala grew older she rarely bought new clothes, yet she was vain enough to methodically scissor out her face from photographs because she believed she had grown ugly. She was greedy as well as sexually voracious.

Dalí was to paint Gala as a mother figure, as an ecstatic Leda ravished by a swan, and dressed in a little girl's sailor suit. Gala was given a thousand nicknames by Dalí, not all complimentary: Olive, Little Lion, Squirrel, Tapir, Bee, My Furry Hazelnut, Leda, Saint Helen . . . Were these chimerical reflections of Gala's true nature or was she, as an accomplice, willing to garb herself in whatever surrealist identity that Dalí created?

In a way, Gala's secrecy was as pronounced as Dalí's colossal exhibitionism. She became adroit at concealing herself behind his showmanship. She entered into his fantastical game, tailoring her image to match the Gala that emerged from Dalí's paintbrush. But the half-lies and distortions she told of her past were, in many ways, as revealing as the truth. They were not extravagant lies but curious camouflages to conceal aspects of her own history she found disturbing or too drab.

Her early life was marked by abrupt changes of fortune and circumstance in which conventionality had to be sacrificed for

11

survival, and her twists of the truth were attempts to flee from this rather plain but painful secret.

When her business associates accused her of hard bargaining, she hinted it was because of her Jewish or Armenian blood. The many aristocrats that Dalí courted came away with the impression that Gala was also touched with nobility. The story circulated that Gala's father managed the vast estate of an enlightened prince, a luxurious sanctuary for free-thinking artists and philosophers. As a baby, Gala once bounced on Count Tolstoy's knee, or so she later claimed. Those amazed by Gala's licentiousness, especially in her later years, were treated with the tale that as a young teenager she had been raped by her stepfather. At times she shifted the story so that it became her brother who raped her. In this version, Gala's stepfather is the hero who banishes the brother to a military academy.

The only bare facts Gala willingly revealed were that she was born Helena Dimitrievna Diakonova in 1895 and that the family lived in Kazan, a university town on the Volga river. The best account of Gala's childhood comes from her younger sister, Lidia Jaroljmec, who laughed off suggestions that their father – or even stepfather, for that matter – had been Jewish or Armenian or the manager of a princely estate.

Gala's real father was a luckless adventurer. Although he came from an educated middle-class background, Diakonov succumbed to the contemporary legend that veins of pure gold gleamed beneath Siberia's ice fields. The tsar was anxious to colonise Siberia, which at that time was a badland of fugitive serfs and trappers, and the discovery of gold was meant to provide a solution. Like many thousands of men in Kazan, Diakonov abandoned his family and went searching for fortune in the other extreme of Russia. Gala was only ten when news reached back from Siberia, 5000 miles away, that her father had died – a pauper.

Aside from Gala, a weak child, her mother Antonia Diakonova was left with a three-year-old daughter, Lidia, two sons, Nikolai and Vadim, and no money. In tsarist Russia a widow was expected to remain in mourning black and was barred by the Russian Orthodox Church from remarrying. Antonia Diakonova flouted convention and incurred the wrath of her relatives by taking the practical step of sharing house with a wealthy lawyer. The couple lived together with Antonia Diakonova's four children. Her two teenage sons, who were old enough to be aware of the social outrage that their mother had committed, detested their new 'stepfather'.

According to Nikolai, her brother, Gala's personality resembled her mother's. 'A petty, mean spirit was alien to Gala. Her vitality was a quality that she inherited from mother. Our mother always had a drive towards living a full life and achieving things.'

Gala could not have known her real father other than through his Siberian letters, but she was old enough to appreciate the step from genteel poverty into a spacious flat with cooks, servants and nannies. She was affectionate with her 'stepfather', perhaps even coquettishly so, following her mother's example. This, however, earned her the animosity of her brothers and sister. Lidia remembers: 'We all fought in the family. Gala was the only one of the four children who liked "stepfather". The rest of us didn't.'

Gala was ridiculed by her siblings because she was so clumsy in the many lessons of tennis, riding, ice-skating, ballet and rowing which the 'stepfather' had anxiously arranged to rid the Diakonov children of their sullenness, though his attempts at buying their affection were futile. 'We all laughed at her because she was bad at sports. Gala was always so slender and fragile. When I was ten and she seventeen, I could carry Gala in my arms from her bath to the bed,' Lidia said.

Nikolai, the younger brother, was locked in ceaseless rebellion against his 'stepfather'. Kola, as he was nicknamed, brought home bad marks from school, and family meals at Christmas or holidays were often marred by bitter rows between the two. The elder brother, Vadim, took refuge in studies and spent a spell in the philology department at Kazan University before the war.

Lidia refused to believe Gala's tales of being sexually abused by either her 'stepfather' or her brother, and it is possible that these were fantasies growing out of Gala's anguish at being caught in the middle of this domestic civil war. Gala's love for her 'stepfather' was treacherous and shameful enough in the eyes of her brothers and sister without Gala having to engage in sexual intercourse with the portly lawyer and family benefactor. On the other hand, it is also equally possible that Lidia was too young to have been privy to such volatile family secrets if they in fact existed.

The parents were not ardent church-goers, and in any case

13

Antonia and her lover would have been unwelcome inside a Russian Orthodox church because of their relationship. Nevertheless the children were given religious instruction at school and only occasionally would the parents' anti-clericalism erupt, such as when Gala and her sister were cautioned against kissing the 'unhygienic' relics in church.

Apart from the family tensions, their life was comfortable. Summer holidays were spent travelling. 'All of us would go, even the nannies. There was always great chaos and confusion at the train station,' recalled Lidia. Sometimes the family boarded the great steam trains that sped them south along the estuary of the Volga to a stately beach resort near Crimea, on the Black Sea. Other times they headed north-west to Finland, where Gala, then in her teens, fell in love for the first time, with a hotel telegraphist. It was not a relationship encouraged by her mother.

Despite its distance from Moscow and St Petersburg, Kazan was not isolated from the intellectual ferment sweeping across Russia at the time. Lenin had been expelled from Kazan University in 1887 for revolutionary activities and banished from the city. He returned a year later and set up a clandestine Marxist study group advocating the overthrow of the tsar. When Lenin was again forced to move on, his disciples remained behind in Kazan, recruiting sympathisers among the university students.

Gala had no interest in politics; that commitment she left to her brother Nikolai, who became the director of a workers' theatre soon after the Revolution. As a female, Gala was banned from attending the university but often turned up for lectures on literature, her passion. Dostoevsky was her favourite Russian writer. Russia was under the cultural sway of France, and this was mirrored in the intellectual finishing school which she and other bright young women of her society were allowed to attend. However much Gala enjoyed literature, she limited her own aspirations to translating other people's poetry and novels from French to Russian.

In a sense, one of her many roles with Dalí was that of translator for his visual language. When art dealers and rich collectors failed to appreciate a new Dalí painting, it was often Gala's persuasiveness that made them eventually see his artistry.

Since childhood, Gala had been plagued by 'something wrong with her neck glands', according to her sister. Later in life, Gala referred to her illness as 'psychic' in origin but this explanation struck her sister Lidia as implausible. 'Gala was always very clear and intelligent. She was the most practical of us all. There was no question of her illness being anything other than physical.' Whatever the reasons, Gala spent much of her childhood in and out of sanatoriums in Moscow. Finally, when her lungs became affected, the doctors feared she would contract tuberculosis, and the family decided to send her to the Clavadel sanatorium near the Davos ski resort in Switzerland for a cure.

Gala was only seventeen when she made the long train journey in 1912, alone and ill, through western Russia, and the Austro-Hungarian empire. Once into Switzerland, Gala changed at Landquart, where she caught a sturdy alpine train that steamed its way up through tunnels that filled with the engine's roar and smoke before the train suddenly emerged into vistas of black fir forests, lakes and snow-covered mountains. It was like nothing Gala had ever before encountered. The health sanatorium, high up in the snow and circled round by crows, was to be her home for the next two years. She had her books, her Dostoevsky and Tolstoy, and when weather permitted she would sink into a deck-chair on the terrace and read voraciously. There were not many young patients in the sanatorium, and it wasn't long before this slender girl with eyes like a mesmerist's caught the attention of a seventeen-year-old French boy, who introduced himself as a poet; immediately, Gala was charmed.

His name was Paul-Eugène Grindel but he called himself Eluard, since he believed Eluard – his grandmother's maiden name – had poetic resonance. This *nom de plume* was also a rebellion against his father, a pragmatic builder who disapproved of his son's effete pastimes.

Paul Eluard was a handsome youth, with big eyes and smooth, earnest features. He dressed in the latest Paris style and wore floppy velvet cravats. His adolescent hands were large and awkward, like gnawed-on bones, and Eluard would clasp them together with a tightness that betrayed his nerves. Much to Gala's distress, a young French girl had begun flirtations with Eluard first. Gala later wrote to Eluard: 'I remember a touching incident at Clavadel when you were getting on "well" with Mademoiselle. . . . I prayed to God, maybe for the first time, for Him to give me the boy that I so adored. And *voilà*, you are mine.'

They were both the same age, and soon began seeing each

other every moment outside the weekly treatment of X-rays, thermometer readings and lung-thumping check-ups with the physicians. The sanatorium had the atmosphere of an ocean liner. There was piano music in the dining room, and the patients passed their time drinking herbal teas and lemonade around little tables where they played cards, traded postage stamps and amused themselves with the latest parlour toy – a 3-D stereoscope which gave an eerie depth to photographs that seemed to parallel the dreamy listlessness of sanatorium life. Gala and Eluard shied away from the others, drawing, and reading the poetry of Walt Whitman, Apollinaire and Baudelaire. A page of their doodles survives. It shows a cubist 'Portrait of a Young Man, The Poet at 17 Years' and a challenging scrawl by Gala: 'Which Young Man?' Eluard has even written down the time for an evening assignation – 10 pm, after the tubercular patients were made to blanket themselves like mummies on their balconies to breathe the sharp night air. Beside this invitation Gala had scrawled: 'I am your disciple.' Their emotions must have been heightened by the dying that went on around them, the stillness that woke them in their separate rooms near dawn when an old man with an irritating cough down the corridor suddenly stopped breathing. The rushing whiteness of the nurses would follow, then the stench of disinfectant as the deceased's room was cleansed. At dawn, Gala and Eluard watched as the body was placed on a special bobsled and disappeared down the snowy slopes to the village mortuary.

Their illness, in a sense, bound them together. Gala's ailment had cocooned her from her family and friends. In this ethereal, tubercular poet she found a perfect understanding for her suffering. Surrounded by piercing alpine beauty, and removed from the stiff parental restraints on courtship, Gala and Paul opened up to each other in a way that would have been impossible back home. They shared favourite poets, dressed as Pierrette and Pierrot, the melancholic clowns, for the sanatorium's masked ball, and even discussed their own virginity. They taught each other coy terms of endearment in each other's languages. Eluard became 'my maltchik dorogoi'; she was his 'belle petite fille'. Soon they were making plans for a life together outside the chandeliered confines of the sanatorium.

A snapshot of them at Clavadel shows Gala perched on the arm of Eluard's chair. She is wearing a woollen turtle-neck and her long auburn hair is braided. Her hands are folded demurely and she is looking across at Eluard. The camera has caught Gala in mid-speech. Her expression is one of concentration, of a lover's earnest response to a fragment of poetry, or of a sense that this photograph would be the first in an album of a lifetime spent together. In contrast, Eluard has chosen to pose with his hair meticulously parted in the middle and with his eyes shut. He looks a dandy, as if he were trying desperately to ape Oscar Wilde, but that at any second the effort would cause him to collapse in laughter.

By 1914 Gala's health had improved enough for her to return, reluctantly, to Russia. Before parting, Eluard proposed an unofficial engagement. They would live in a country house, far enough outside Paris for the air to be healthy but close enough to enjoy the city's art galleries and theatres. Eluard had published several poems by then, but sensibly promised Gala that he would swallow his pride and work for his father's building firm until he could live off his writing. The prospect of abandoning Russia and the security of her family to marry an under-aged poet in a foreign country did not scare her. For all of her practicality, Gala time after time allowed herself to be governed by her emotions. She grasped at Eluard's proposal.

Their declaration of love, however, was overshadowed by the outbreak of war. Gala's train clattered out of the Swiss mountains and crossed the Austrian border just as the mighty Habsburg Empire was preparing for battle with Russia. The heir to the Austro-Hungarian throne, Archduke Franz Ferdinand, had been assassinated in June 1914 in Sarajevo, and when the Habsburg armies went to punish the Serbians, the Russians were obliged to defend their Serbian allies. Germany was then dragged in by the Habsburgs to fight off the Russians, and it was not long before France, Britain and eventually 90 per cent of the western world's population were at the Great War's mercy.

Gala arrived back in Kazan rattled, but unharmed, by several days' delay on the railway, as trains were commandeered to transport war supplies and troops to the Russian frontier. Her homecoming was saddened by the news that her older brother Vadim, had been recruited out of university into an officers' training school.

The geographical gap between Gala and Eluard seemed to stretch wider with war, and Gala grew desperate. Her behaviour

17

so worried her stepfather that he considered seeking medical advice. Her sister recalls: 'Gala even started to get a temperature out of sheer longing for him.' Gala rejected potential suitors arranged by her parents. Of this period she later wrote: 'I never kissed a man; I suspected them all and mocked them when they tried to be sweet to me.'

Her anxiety over Eluard increased when word arrived that he had been drafted into the French army. Once Prussia's force was turned on Russia, France foolishly decided to pounce on coveted German borderland. Eluard's poor health kept him from the trenches. Instead, he was made a hospital orderly, serving near the Somme battlefield, where there were days when thousands of fresh casualties would be carted in.

France and Russia were allies and were able to keep postal links open by sidestepping enemy territory through various circuitous routes. Eluard and Gala wrote regularly, but sometimes weeks passed before they received a letter from each other. The delays were made all the more agonising by news dispatches from the battlefield. Russian troops were defeated by the Germans at Tannenburg (now Poland), and only the aid of 2000 Parisian taxi cabs, speeding soldiers to the Battle of the Marne, managed to halt the German conquest of France. Thousands of miles of barbed wire were being unrolled, from the North Sea down to the mountains of neutral Switzerland, separating Gala from her young poet. If anything, the futility of their situation strengthened their will to reunite. Gala pestered and pleaded with her parents to let her travel to France, and even went on a virtual hunger strike. Her sister Lidia recalls, 'Gala didn't eat or drink. She only wanted to go back to him.'

In their letters Gala and Eluard worked out possible sea and rail routes that she might take to reach him. It was dangerous going, all the more so because of Gala's poor health, but the trip was not impossible. The only way was through a complicated series of train changes which would take her either to Sweden or to a Russian port on the Baltic. From there Gala's sea voyage to France would have been reasonably safe; Britain's naval superiority in the North Sea kept the German warships at bay. The political climate at home also favoured Gala's departure. Strikes and famines had erupted because of the wartime privations, and the Russian defeat at Tannenburg – the commanding officer, General Alexander Samsonov, had wandered off into the woods and shot himself when the battle turned against him – all heightened discontent against the tsarist regime. If the trip to France was perilous, so too was staying at home.

Finally, in the summer of 1916, when Gala was twenty-one, her parents relented and allowed her to leave Kazan to marry Eluard. They had never met their daughter's future husband. As Gala embarked on her journey, her brother Nikolai teased her for being 'an old virgin' because so many Russian girls were married off in their teens. There were easier ways of losing her virginity than by travelling through central Europe at the height of war to join her lover, whose chances of survival seemed to dim with every grim communiqué from the French battlefield.

3

A Poet Under Fire

In August 1916 Gala arrrived in Paris with a trunk full of weighty Russian novels, her smartest clothes, some pocket money from her stepfather, and without a clue as to how to keep house or hold a job. She soon found that her broken French did not equip her to earn a living as a translator, as she had hoped.

Paris was far closer to the battlefield than Kazan had been, and Gala found a city under the shadow of war. Cubist artists were designing camouflage netting for big cannons. Newspapers were filled with glowing communiqués from the front, heroic anecdotes of men – and dogs – fighting against the barbaric Boches, and advertisements for reeds that would make the murky trench water drinkable. Such inventions as submarines, zeppelins and aeroplanes, which before had seemed as harmless as fairground rides, were pitted in bizarre combat that seemed to rumble out of the pages of H. G. Wells's *War of the Worlds*. To the war correspondents these inventions seemed as awesome as sea monsters. Artificial legs were being brought by the shipload from America, and the Académie Française was offering a great prize for an ode to France. Eluard was not among the contestants. Disgusted by the carnage witnessed at his Somme field hospital, Eluard took refuge in the pacifist literature that trickled to the front.

Russians were in vogue – merchants, diplomats, musicians and even soldiers; a token regiment of Cossacks fought alongside the French. It was considered patriotic to buy Russian war bonds, and Eluard's parents were among the thousands of Frenchmen who did so – much to their regret later. Even Parisian fashion came under Slavic influence. Cossack hats were the rage even in warm September, along with sensible linen dresses with bibs that a woman could wear while spotting German zeppelins in the countryside or bandaging wounded soldiers. The popularity of things Russian was not lost on Gala. At her superior education school in Kazan she had dabbled in art. Once it became apparent that she could not translate, Gala toyed with the idea of becoming a fashion designer under the tutelage of Madame Grindel, who was a seamstress. However, her future mother-in-law seems to have quashed the idea.

The Somme was a day's train journey from Paris, and the French military command was fairly tolerant about granting occasional leave to the soldiers. Eluard had secured a furlough for Gala's arrival. Despite their steady correspondence, Gala and Eluard must have been anxious about the reunion. They were nineteen when they parted; now they were twenty-one. Of the two, Eluard was the more altered by their two-year estrangement. The war had transformed the dilettante poet and had made him morbid. As he wrote to his mother soon before Gala's arrival: 'The cannons sound ceaselessly. . . . In the past three days, we have received, treated and evacuated nearly 4000 wounded. What a state they're in. The cemetery is filled. Only miracles keep some of the wounded alive. This war is misery, misery. We now have an extra ambulance for surgery. We cut and we cut.'

Gala too must have had doubts about the sanity of abandoning Russia for Eluard. These doubts surfaced in her letters to Eluard at the Somme, revealing a frantic craving for the reassurance of Eluard's love. It was a response that demanded much of Eluard at a time when his own mind echoed with the screams of wounded soldiers. Their relationship had flourished in the rarefied atmosphere of the Swiss sanatorium – without the intrusion of parents – but, once in France, Gala found herself at the mercy of Eluard's possessive mother. Madame Jeanne-Marie Cousin Grindel had the worry of having both her only son and her husband away at war, and her veneer of hospitality towards Gala often wore thin. Madame Grindel recognised that Gala was a 'good Russian' but as spoiled and dreamy as her own pampered son. Though the match may have seemed unsuitable, Madame Grindel was too pliant a mother to actively oppose Eluard's wishes of marriage. Throughout her life Gala found it easier to befriend men than women, and this seems true with Eluard's parents; Gala ingratiated herself with Eluard's father.

Even in wartime, it was considered improper for a boy and a

girl to lodge under the same roof, but, faced with this lovesick immigrant, Eluard's parents had no option but to take her in with them in their flat on the rue Ordener, near the Sacré-Cœr. Eluard and Gala solemnly declared their wish to be married as soon as possible.

He instructed his mother to prepare a ceremony that would be similar to Gala's 'act of birth' in its purity: 'You must do all that is necessary . . . arrange for the wedding announcement and buy the white gown for Gala – Gala and I are of age, and we've been engaged for the past four years. Our simple union will not change the conditions of our life and, the main thing, it will not injure nor deceive anyone. Our civil and religious marriage will be like all other marriages in these wretched times of great war.' This cryptic remark about not deceiving or injuring anyone seemed to signal the defiance with which Eluard flaunted Gala before his parents. It was as if to say, how can you stand in our way? Ours is the one honest and innocent gesture possible amidst the senselessness of war.

Judging from Gala's letters to Eluard, it seems that during that first month, late at night while his parents slept, the two became lovers for the first time. Remaining virgins must have seemed an absurdity when the chance existed that Eluard might be killed before their wedding night. However much Eluard had dreamed of making love to Gala, in any number of different fashions, he was not prepared for Gala's exuberance and sexual inventiveness. Back at the front, Eluard began to brood. Finally, he reproached Gala with having learned her tricks from another man. In reply, Gala assured him that '*Never* after our meeting [in the Swiss sanatorium] was I with someone the way I was with you.' In a following letter, she added:

Despise me and insult me, but not my love. . . . I have only my love, [the desire] for you to possess me entirely. There is no uncleanliness in my thoughts or my ideas, not in reality, not in my life or my feelings. If I do everything with you – even 'strange things' – I'm certain that because I love you. All is pure, beautiful and right.

Right now I'm *absolutely* chaste and pure. I haven't done anything to displease you, not one gesture or one thought, not one movement or one word. . . . I don't hide anything from you. My life is clear and all that I do is for you. Ask your mother if you have any doubts. I don't know anyone [in Paris], and I don't go out apart from my [French] lessons. I don't receive any letters from ANYONE other than my parents.

Once Eluard's short furlough had ended, Gala moved into his room. She wrote of feeling a psychic connection with him and worried over his welfare to the point that she hardly slept. She wore Eluard's green sweater as a kind of protective charm. Gala gamely tried to befriend Madame Grindel. They strolled together in the Bois de Boulogne, and Gala tried to busy herself helping Madame Grindel with her chores. Both Madame Grindel and her husband came from modest homes and had grown prosperous through hard work. From the first moment that Madame Grindel took Gala into the kitchen, it was obvious to her that Gala, who had been waited on by servants in Kazan, had no idea of how to cook or keep house for her future husband.

Her response to the strangeness of her new surroundings and the absence of Eluard was, in her words, 'to try and think myself very small and hide in the simple, ordinary things, the daily tasks'. She knitted Eluard a green headscarf for the approaching winter and sent him cloth samples of the new red, black and gold dress she was making to be beautiful for his homecoming. Her letters are filled with gay chatter – the red armchairs she would like to buy for his study, the naughty purchase of Coty perfume which she promises not to use until Eluard's return, and the dreary French philosophers she is reading to improve herself. One senses that this prattle, mixed in with fierce avowals of love, was Gala's recipe for helping Eluard to forget about the war, however momentarily.

Gala, who according to her sister never guarded any secret ambitions, confided once to Eluard: 'I'll never have the appearance of a housewife, I'll be a proper coquette (bright, perfumed and with manicured hands). I'll read a lot, a lot. I'll work in design or translation. I'll do everything but have the air of a woman who doesn't exert herself.'

There were times when Gala's cheerfulness shattered, when her worry over Eluard's safety and her own self-doubts about being in France left her bedridden and morose. She was so distracted that once at the dinner table she bit her tongue as she sipped soup, and Madame Grindel scolded her. Gala came to detest Eluard's mother. She discovered that Madame Grindel

23

would chalk a line on the jam jar so she could catch Gala sneaking more jam than she was entitled to. 'This drove me wild,' Gala later recounted to a friend. 'We Russians like to put jam in our afternoon tea. This woman was so mean-minded.' Once she ventured out alone to Bourget, on the edge of Paris, by tram. She wanted to be alone, and took a single seat at the rear of the first car, too absorbed to notice if anyone sat across from her.

I was very tired and sad. I thought of all that was saddest in my anxious life (!!!) – when I was a little girl it was the 'sadness' of my parents. Then our separation, our sickness, our Love, etc., etc. And I thought of what awaits me.

I was completely lost and submerged in myself. Then all of a sudden I heard the monstrous laughter of a crowd. The sound was behind me on the platform – men howled with laughter, and there was one high and piercing voice of a 'single' woman that irritated me the most. . . . I detested the cries, the crowd, the noise behind me. And I loved the tramway, the machine, quiet and impassive, without the 'disgusting' shouts.

For the most part, though, it seems Gala deliberately set out to distract Eluard from the war with a balm of mundane details. Her letters did not succeed in their purpose. In November, Eluard asked to be transferred from the safety of his hospital job to the infantry. Gala was stunned and angry. Eluard's decision had nothing to do with any sudden upsurge of patriotism; he was still deeply opposed to the war. His desire for combat seems to have arisen out of self-doubt, of being guilty of the 'shame of cowardice'. He wrote to Gala, 'I plead with you, let me lead a life that's harder and less servile.' Curiously, his brooding over cowardice arose just a few days after voicing his suspicions about Gala's fidelity. It seems as though Eluard, in a way, was chastising himself for doubting Gala.

His self-doubt must have been terrible because Eluard, from his hospital view at Hargicourt, had excruciating knowledge of what dangers awaited him as an infantryman in the trenches. The Somme was the bloodiest battle in all history. Four months before, in July 1916, the French Field-Marshal Joseph Joffre decided to hurl French and British troops at what seemed the weakest point of the German line – the Somme. The Germans,

including a young corporal named Adolf Hitler, were dug deep
in their trenches and ready for the Allied attack. On the first
charge, the French and British lost nearly 100,000 men. At best,
the Allies conquered 1000 yards of enemy ground that day. The
assault dragged on for several months, with such monstrous
weapons as tanks and poisonous gas scything across the battlefield for the first time. The Allied command persisted with their
orders to attack 'without intermission', and wave after wave of
soldiers were mowed down by German machine-guns. Heavy
rains came, and in the trenches soldiers drowned in the muddy
torrents. The final toll was over 1.2 million German and Allied
soldiers dead. It was not the glamour of war Eluard wanted but
redempton.

This sacrifice was not one that Gala wanted him to suffer. She
did not understand Eluard's reasons and accused him of 'banal
arrogance'. In a letter she addressed to her 'Dear Husband'
(though they were not yet married) the fierce and obstinate side
of Gala's character emerges. She bullies, insults and belittles
him; she plays the wronged woman with sulphurous intensity.
'Maybe you haven't noticed,' she begins sarcastically, 'but I have
done and do much for you. All my life, all my spirit, my blood,
I have consecrated to you. Not all women would do that. If you
go [into the infantry] . . . it will be as if you rejected me, my
very life.' How could Eluard value his own pride and his fear of
appearing cowardly over love, she asks. 'I don't dare plead with
you. I feel like a poor small woman that one loves when one lacks
anything more "grand" or "serious" to do. . . . I had dreams of
resting this week, of reading tranquilly. It's impossible. If only
you knew how I'm suffering. I feel that you don't love me, that
I'm helpless, that you're incapable of doing anything grand for
me. You're like all these other arrogant young men, carried away
by the stupid enthusiasms of the crowd. I came [to France]
hoping to calm your suffering. And have I made a mistake?'

She ends her tirade by threatening to abandon Eluard and
become a nurse for wounded Russian soldiers, which she admits
would be a slow form of suicide. 'It's dangerous for my health,
but if you don't love me the way I want – not enough, that is –
I'll be absolutely crushed. And since I don't have the courage to
kill myself off in one blow, I'll wear myself out slowly. These are
my "threats" [from a previous letter]. Believe me, I'll do it. I'm
just as energetic as you above all in my despair. You're not

rational. It's useless for me to be in Paris.' She signed off: 'Gala, your little unhappy girl.'

Unfortunately, Eluard's reply has been lost. It must have soothed Gala, however, for any further threats of donning a nurse's uniform were absent from her next missive, in which she chatted about Russian books and the maid's three-day holiday and contented herself with the dark phrase: 'Don't act. You can't even imagine how serious is what you're doing to me.'

Eluard, however, was not to be dissuaded from joining the infantry. So Gala again resorted to emotional blackmail. She revived the idea of nursing for the specific purpose of making herself 'definitely ill'. She explained: 'You mustn't forget that I'm hysterical and that, for my age and for my physical strength I'm too, too nervous. The slightest things put me beside myself and anything that has to do with you renders me absolutely crazy.' Mixed in with her genuine concern for Eluard's safety, there was a kind of spitefulness in Gala. It is almost as though she was angry with him for jeopardising her cosy dream of creative bliss together by making himself a target for the German sharp-shooters. Having made the sacrifice of leaving Russia for him, she expected an equal test of faith from Eluard, namely that he abandon his notion of experiencing some nebulous 'hope' on the battlefield.

The two showed very different views of love. Gala's was more optimistic; she focused her thoughts on being with Eluard after the war's end, the kind of furniture that would decorate their apartment, the gowns and the perfume with which she would seduce him. Eluard's love, in contrast, was so enveloped by the war that he did not allow himself the luxury of imagining that the cannon fire would ever cease. His love for Gala sustained him but did not, he believed, grant him the right to be spared death on the battlefield. Thousands of soldiers lay dying at the Somme with the talisman of a girlfriend's love letter in their pockets.

On 28 December 1916 Eluard's papers arrived authorising his transfer to the 95th Infantry Regiment. The poet had traded in his syringes and first-aid bandages for a rifle and bayonet. Not surprisingly, Gala did not carry out her threat of becoming a nurse for the Russian battalion in France. She pinned her hopes on a swift end to the war and Eluard's return.

Eluard's entering the infantry quickened their resolve to marry.

As a Russian, Gala faced difficulties in obtaining the proper certificates for their marriage. Gala, in particular, wanted to be married in church and was in a quandary about whether it would be 'sinful' for the ceremony to be conducted by a Catholic priest instead of a Russian Orthodox clergyman. 'For me,' she wrote to Eluard, seeking his advice, 'it's the same being a Catholic or Orthodox as long as I'm a believer. And I believe deeply. That's why (the only reason why) I absolutely want to get married in a church. The beginning of our life together is a very serious moment for me and I want God to bless our love.'

· Eluard was more concerned that Gala would find him ugly with his hair shaved off for the army.

At best, Eluard could secure only four days' leave. Two days were to be wasted shuffling between various offices of the army, the church and the government for permission to be married. He wrote to his mother: 'No one should be invited, given the lack of time and the impossibility of inviting everyone. . . . All that I want is simply to be united civilly and Christianly.'

Gala had plans for their honeymoon, their 'poor little two days'. She wrote: 'I can't stop thinking about our days . . . of intimacy – absolutely alone all day and all night. We won't go out at all, or maybe just for an hour or so, for an agreeable walk in the fresh morning.' Gala also made it clear that for those two days before their wedding she expected Eluard to remain chaste. The streets around his army training barracks teemed with whores. When Eluard protested that he could withstand their temptations, Gala replied: 'I believe you absolutely – I'm not afraid [of these] women. I know that two enormous forces – me and God – will suffice to hold back these attractions – hardly seductive – because the women over there are too vice-ridden, too dirty and too womanly [for Eluard's liking].'

In February 1917, in the white wedding dress chosen by Eluard's mother, Gala was married. Soon after, Eluard was to enthuse of Gala:

> Her eyes are always open
> And she will not let me sleep.
> Her dreams in full light
> Make the suns evaporate,
> Make me laugh, cry and laugh,
> Talk without having anything to say.

27

It wasn't long before the intensity of Gala's desires made many of Eluard's own dreams evaporate.

4

Agile Incest

Never, in all of her letters to Eluard at the front, did Gala once mention having children. In her domestic daydreams, Gala fancied herself as a sweetly scented wife and lover. She saw herself arranging flowers, perhaps, or perched on the arm of Eluard's chair reading the first draft of a love poem. Motherhood seemed alien to Gala, possibly because after their two-year separation all she wanted was to recapture the romance of their youth. This was not to happen. Gala and Eluard were married on his furlough from the army in February 1917, and by late August Gala was pregnant. It could have happened on Eluard's second or even first leave from the front as a married soldier.

Gala was extraordinarily wilful, and her pregnancy – if indeed it was an accident, as it seems – may have been one of the rare events in her life over which she had no control. This, in part, may explain her coolness to her daughter, Cécile. Being a mother never fitted into Gala's image of herself, glittering and free.

Eluard still had another two years of military service and Gala continued living with his parents. Relations grew strained over a financial matter. The Grindels had invested heavily in Russian war bonds and they lost this considerable sum when the tsar was overthrown. Irrationally, Madame Grindel blamed Gala for the loss, as she pounced on anything that proved – to her mind – that she was an unsuitable wife for her only son. Gala confided to her sister, Lidia, incredulously: 'Madame Grindel never forgave me for the war bonds. She thought it was all my fault.' Once Gala gave birth to Cécile, Madame Grindel would have unlimited opportunity to twist less imaginary grievances to her advantage against Gala.

The Russian Revolution also heightened Gala's sense of

isolation from her own family. The post seldom arrived from Russia but when it did the news was usually bad. Revolutionaries had deemed the family's flat too big and bourgeois. Servants were dismissed and peasants allowed to squat inside the flat. Gala's family were squeezed into one and a half rooms. Then word reached Gala that her eldest brother, Vadim, who had come home ill and exhausted from officers' school, had quietly died in a corner of their overrun flat. Her Russian stepfather told Gala, with good reason, that she was far better off in Paris.

Eluard rushed back from the front for Gala's delivery. In a note to a friend, he wrote: 'On Saturday evening, I attended the arrival to the world, very simply, of a beautiful small girl, Cécile, my daughter, to present her to you.'

If Gala felt any disillusionment over bearing a child so soon after her marriage, she did not convey any such sentiment to her family in Russia. 'At last you have a granddaughter,' she wrote to her mother, who had often chided her for waiting until she was an 'old maid' of twenty-two before getting married.

In some ways, Eluard's parents exacted a toll, though a fairly reasonable one, for putting up with Gala and the new baby. When Eluard was demobilised in 1919, he and Gala moved into a flat in Saint-Brice paid for by his father. It was understood that Eluard, in exchange, would join his father in a new business venture, developing a housing estate in the Paris suburbs. The young poet felt the responsibilities of parenthood closing in on him. In 1918, under a pseudonym, he had published *Poems for Peace*, in which one sees how his war experiences had steeled his love for Gala. Eluard yearned to write, not build houses. His frustration was evident in the street names he choose for the estate: Marquis de Sade, Lautréamont, Balzac, Apollinaire.

There is no correspondence showing how Gala might have coped with nursing a new child, changing nappies and offering solace to a husband who, trapped in a smothering job, tried to write at night and at weekends. Madame Grindel had maids and a large house where Gala, had she wanted to, could have deposited Cécile and skipped off to Paris with Eluard. Perhaps she did just that; but one senses an early battle of wills between Gala and her mother-in-law. Gala desperately wanted to prove her worth as a wife to Eluard, and show that all the promises and domestic dreams she wrote of would come true. However much Gala desired freedom to be with Eluard it is doubtful that she would have suffered her daughter to be handed over to Madame Grindel.

After office hours, away from the blueprints and account ledgers, Eluard's life began to find literary focus. There was an artistic impatience shared by Eluard and others of his generation who had returned from the trenches with a deep distrust for the political structure which had wreaked such devastation across Europe. The alternative was to be found, they believed, either through the example of the Russian Revolution – whose ideas had inflamed the working classes from the coalmines of Yorkshire to Marseille docks – or, in the cultural sphere, through the negative anarchy proposed by a monocled Romanian, Tristan Tzara. The latter movement was called Dadaism.

At the time, the leading acolytes of Tzara were three Frenchmen – all in their twenties – who ran an arts review called *Littérature*. Eluard submitted pieces to the review and soon befriended its editors, André Breton, Louis Aragon and Philippe Soupault. Breton brought Tzara down from Switzerland to Paris and the review jettisoned many of its more staid contributors such as André Gide and Blaise Cendrars. Eluard learned that Aragon's wife, Elsa, was also a Russian, but she and Gala were too alike, too haughty and hard, for friendship to flower.

Littérature also had its eye on new painters – Breton 'discovered' Marcel Duchamp – and Eluard acted as a talent scout, mainly because he was the only one with enough cash to buy the paintings of such 'new' artists as Pablo Picasso and Joan Miró. One of the more daring galleries was Au Sans Pareil, and it was there, in May 1920, that Eluard for the first first time saw the Dadaist collages of the German artist Max Ernst. Corseted ladies grew lions' heads, assassins flew on angels' wings, and trees sprouted from horses' backs. Word had also reached back from Cologne that Ernst and Hans Arp had staged an exhibition where the entrance was through a public lavatory.

Eluard was so taken by Ernst's bizarre collages that he travelled to his studio in Cologne to coax him into moving to Paris. Eluard's immediate and lasting friendship with Ernst was to alter for ever his own marriage to Gala.

In the summer of 1922, Gala and Eluard trekked to a Dadaist colony set up on a farm high in the Austrian Alps. Ernst was there with his wife, Lou, and their two-year-old son, Jimmy. Lou Ernst did not like Gala and felt immediately threatened by her –

31

with good reason. It was not long before Ernst was slipping out of his bed in the farmhouse to join Gala and Eluard down the hall in theirs. The affair did not escape the notice of the Dadaist residents. When a group from the farm went on a naked romp in a nearby mountain lake, Ernst and Gala behaved without inhibition. Eluard seemed to enjoy this. As Tzara later told Pierre Argillet, a Paris art dealer: 'Eluard liked group sex. He was keen for his friends to make love to Gala – while he watched or joined in.'

Max's Jewish wife was less amused. She had been ostracised by her wealthy family for marrying Ernst. When Lou confronted her husband, he confessed that he found Gala more 'passionate' than her. Not surprisingly, she grew to hate Gala, 'that Russian female . . . that slithering, glittering creature with dark falling hair, vaguely oriental with luminant black eyes and small delicate bones, who had to remind one of a panther. This almost silent, avaricous woman, who, having failed to entice her husband into an affair with me in order to get Max, finally decided to keep both men, with Eluard's loving consent.'

When she tried to gain Eluard's support in halting the affair, his response stunned her. 'You must understand,' Eluard told Lou, 'that I love Max Ernst much more than Gala. . . . You don't know what it is like to be married to a Russian woman.' This rather coy evasion hides the fact that Eluard was obviously delighted with the situation.

Tensions between Lou and the threesome soured the other Dadaists' idyll. Tzara thought the fault was entirely Gala's. As he complained to an American guest, Matthew Josephson, a social historian: 'Of course we don't give a damn about what they do, or who sleeps with whom. But why must that Gala make it such a Dostoevsky drama? It's boring, it's insufferable, unheard of!'

Eluard persuaded Ernst that great things were afoot. In the 1920s the limits of man and the universe had been stretched by scientific discovery. Freud had explored the territory of dreams; Einstein's theory of relativity had been proved by a lunar eclipse. The war, Dada and the Russian Revolution had all threatened to shake the very political foundations, or so they believed. All that remained, Eluard told Ernst, was to detonate a similar explosion in art. Ernst was needed on *Littérature*, Eluard said, for he had 'buried old Reason, the curse of so many disorders . . . through the free representation of a liberated universe'. So Ernst prepared to leave for Paris, after telling his wife: 'I would like very much to be happily married to you. But it is just not working.' He left her and his son, Jimmy, in poverty; even after Ernst's departure, her strict Jewish family refused to take her back.

With Ernst and Eluard, it was an attraction of opposites. Eluard was quiet and considered, Ernst fairly reckless. In recounting their war stories, the two men found that they had faced each other across the trenches and had possibly exchanged shots. Three years after the war Eluard wrote, 'We became the best friends in the world and together we fight intensely for the same cause, that of man's total emancipation.' Ernst was an attractive man, blonder than Eluard, with blue eyes and an ironic smile. He agreed to go to Paris, but there was one hitch: word of Ernst's scandalous antics with the German Dadaists had reached back to the French authorities. They had heard about his exhibition in a public lavatory. Another time, Ernst had armed gallery-goers with hatchets to destroy any pictures they did not like. The smashing was punctuated by a young girl in a white communion gown who recited obscene poems. Not surprisingly, the French denied his visa application.

Such was Eluard's dedication to his new German friend that he contrived to smuggle Ernst into France illegally on his own passport. Had he been caught, Eluard might have landed himself in gaol. Breton and the other editors were just as enthusiastic over Ernst's art as Eluard had been. They gave him work illustrating *Littérature* with his sardonic collages, but it was scarcely enough for Ernst to survive on. Without the proper identification he could not find a steady job, and so Eluard magnanimously invited Ernst to live with him, Gala and Cécile. His adulation of Ernst was infectious and he flourished their friendship like a banner. In the beginning, at least, he wanted Gala to love Ernst as much as he did. Eluard was to regret this.

As well as being a painter, Ernst was a sculptor and poet whose riotous energy brightened up Gala's rather solitary daily existence in the suburbs. He would return from Paris full of anecdotes about his picaresque misadventures trying to earn a few francs. Once, while acting as a film extra on the set of *The Three Musketeers*, Ernst felt too hot inside his armour and wriggled out of it on camera, ruining a costly battle scene; he was sacked.

At weekends, as well as painting he delighted Gala by crafting fantastic jewellery for her and toys for Cécile.

Leaving Cécile behind, the threesome once made a pilgrimage to Giorgio de Chirico's studio in Rome. The Italian painter was amused at having been discovered by the Paris surrealists, and at first he treated them cordially. It was made clear to de Chirico that Gala was his for the taking. He did not refuse her, though, as he later explained to Pierre Argillet, he did not relish the idea of a foursome in bed. 'De Chirico was very independent, and after a while their presence began to annoy him,' said Argillet. 'De Chirico told them: "Look, why are you always hanging around my studio? Go and tour around Rome." ' 'Master, we have come here to see only you and your paintings,' replied Eluard. After that, de Chirico tossed them out. He thought of keeping Gala, but when he found out that she couldn't even boil an egg he sent her away too.

However, de Chirico later gave Gala two untitled canvases, which she valued among her favourites.

Once Ernst had moved in with the Eluards, many more friends and artists flocked out to their suburban home in Saint-Brice. Among so many revolutionaries, Eluard was a little ashamed of his wealth; it raised embarrassing questions about his bourgeois employment with his father. Breton had dropped out of medical school to practise his art full-time and only Eluard held down a job in the family firm. Gala became a centre of attention, and she enjoyed it. The two most fashionable dress designers, Schiaparelli and Coco Chanel, vied with each other to dress Gala in their creations. Gala played the designers off against each other, wheedling outfits from them for nothing. She preferred Chanel.

At first the three lived happily under one roof. Saint-Brice grew too small for them, and Eluard found a big villa for them in Eaubonne, near the forest of Montmorency. Eluard had dutifully chosen a neighbourhood close to his parents' house in Montlignon. It had a garden, and Gala made much of raising chickens. Ernst repaid the Eluards for the lodging by painting the entire house from floor to ceiling with frescos. The two friends travelled together by train into Paris: Eluard would go to his father's property office, Ernst to the toy workshop where he hammered out novelties. Gala stayed at home with her daughter.

In one of her few interviews, Cécile told a Spanish journalist: 'When I was a girl, my father seemed very far away. He was always going to his surrealist meetings in Paris. . . . I stayed alone in the garden. My mother would say: "Go and play in the garden." ' With its high stone wall and dark, oppressive forest of trees, the garden offered her no solace, only a feeling of being lost, trapped. 'I ended up hating that garden,' she said bitterly, 'and the countryside. I ended up hating everything.' The Eaubonne house, with its dreamlike jungle interior of colour, may have been a lush sanctuary from the adults' daily drudgery, but for young Cécile it too was a nightmare. 'The exterior of the house was very banal. But the inside was fantastic and strange. All the rooms were filled with surrealist paintings, even in my room, my parents' bedroom, the salon. Everywhere. Some of these paintings made me frightened. In the dining room, for example, there was a naked woman with her entrails showing in very vivid colours. I was eight at the time, and those images made me very, very afraid.' Cécile took refuge in reading fairytales, as though searching in her imagination for some happy ending to her solitude, one which was denied her by her parents. 'I didn't have any brothers or sisters or cousins or friends. I was so lonely,' she said.

Weekends at Eaubonne seemed like a gathering of gullible spiritualists. Eluard was more a follower than a leader; when André Breton – a leonine-looking patriarch who dressed in green clothes and smoked a green pipe – rejected Dadaism, Eluard followed suit. Dadaism was beginning to seem more like a childish tantrum than a liberation of the spirit. They were searching for something else, a 'language of the soul'. They dabbled in automatic writing, read tarot cards, held seances and interpreted each other's dreams. Gala drifted about the house dressed in the long silk robes of a high priestess or a witch who was not always benign. She was fascinated by tarot cards; later, she cast Dalí's cards ritually every morning. One poet, Robert Desnos, would writhe around the Eluards' living room in a trance which was a prelude to his automatic writing. With the backdrop of Ernst's frescos, they must have seemed like characters floating about in a surrealist painting.

A word was needed to describe this movement, to set it apart from Dada and all that had come before. The term 'surrealist' had first appeared in Guillaume Apollinaire's 1917 play, *Les Mamelles de Tirésias*. It is not known whether it was Breton himself who borrowed the word from Apollinaire, but he gave definition to it in the *Surrealist Manifesto* of 1924:

> Thought dictated in the absence of all control exerted by reason, and outside all aesthetic or moral preoccupations. . . .
> Surrealism is based on the belief in the superior reality of certain forms of association heretofore neglected, in the omnipotence of the dream, and in the disinterested play of thought. It leads to the permanent destruction of all other psychic mechanisms and to its substitution for them in the solution of the principal problems of life.

Breton admonished his followers to 'drop everything . . . take to the roads', and that is exactly what Eluard did. After correcting the final proofs for a book of melancholic poems, *Mourir de ne pas mourir* ('To Die of Not Dying'), Eluard did the next best thing: he disappeared.

On 24 March 1924 Eluard's father received a telegram from his son, who had removed 17,000 francs from the bank. Robert Valette, a biographer of Eluard, described the poet as endowed 'with an almost feminine softness while [nevertheless] being capable of a rage and violence that is almost insane.' This rage burns through in the telegram to his father:

> Dear father, I've had enough. I'm leaving on a trip. I'm dropping all the business affairs that you've undertaken for me. . . . Don't put the police or the private detectives on my trail. The first one who gets in my way, I'll make sure he won't be in a state to bother me again. And that will be bad for the honour of your name.
> In general, here is what it would be best for you to say: to *everyone*. I had a haemorrhage on arriving in Paris, I'm now in a clinic and then you'll say that I'm in a Swiss sanatorium.
> Make the biggest efforts for Gala and Cécile.
>
> Eugène [Eluard's real name]

Eluard had sent the telegram before boarding a train for Holland to begin a journey around the globe to the Antilles, Panama, Tahiti, the Cook Islands, New Zealand, Australia, Java, Sumatra, Indochina and Ceylon. It seems that the first Gala heard about his departure was from his distraught father, clutching the telegram.

Robert Valette suggests that another reason for Eluard's journey, apart from following Breton's call to vagabondage, was that he felt trapped by working with his father. There is every indication, though, that Eluard's departure was a flight of pique, brought on by Gala's affair with Max Ernst; he had begun to feel excluded from Gala and Ernst's relationship.

Eluard's self-imposed exile, seen in this light, may have been provoked by jealousy and anguish at watching Gala's fondness for Ernst grow. His own relationship with Gala would have been under threat. In a poem entitled *Max Ernst*, Eluard writes:

> In a corner agile incest
> turns around the virginity of a white robe.

Charles Whiting, a critic writing in *The French Review*, said: 'It is difficult not to see that the incest [of the poem] refers to the quasi-fraternal relationship between Eluard and Ernst, while the virginity and the white robe here are typical expressions of Eluard's vision of Gala.'

How willing an adultress was Gala? Some believe that it was Eluard's licentiousness that corrupted her, that he pushed her into the arms of other men for his own prurient interest and to justify his own infidelities. But Gala, for all her youthful naïvety, was a woman of strong character. It is difficult to believe that anyone, even her earnest poet/husband, could have lured her into sexual permissiveness if she was not willing. Eluard condoned it; she undoubtedly enjoyed it. She later told a friend, Henri Pastoureau, that at Eaubonne she, Ernst and Eluard had slept together in the same bed, every night. 'She explained that, to her great regret, it wasn't anatomically possible for her to be sodomised.' Gala did not elaborate on this, but perhaps she found it too painful.

Denise Tual, a film maker, once accompanied the trio on a skiing holiday in the Austrian Alps. 'It was plain that Gala was definitely with Eluard *and* Ernst.' Tual, who disliked Gala, added: 'I don't think it took Ernst long to see through Gala. He painted her coiled around with an ugly snake. He saw her all right.'

Tual also remembers Gala flirting with Jacques Prévert, 'sharing strange language jokes', on the skiing holiday.

Instead of fighting to regain Gala, Eluard reacted with a petulant gallantry, leaving the field clear for his rival. It was a pattern that he would repeat later with Dalí. However, his apparent nonchalance concealed a profound emotional crisis. Shortly after his disappearance, Eluard wrote of losing 'his capacity for loving', and also wrote that 'Alone, the head is dead, my face doesn't understand me any more.'

The cover story that Eluard had thoughtfully provided to explain his disappearance did not hold. Eluard's father told Gala what had happened, she told Ernst, and together the two of them spread the news to the other surrealists. Eluard's voyage was considered by them to be heroic. He was hailed as a 'new Rimbaud' after the young genius who abandoned poetry in his early twenties and squandered the rest of his life – quite admirably, thought the surrealists – on the Horn of Africa.

Had he told Gala of his plan beforehand, Eluard's disappearance would have lost its shock value. She might even have succeeded in stopping him, using the same combination of cajoling and cooing shown in her early letters to him during the war. Her reaction to Eluard's emotional oneupmanship was curious: she did not grovel to get him back, nor did she want to cut him off. In the meantime, Gala faced the difficult task of explaining to Eluard's parents why he might have vanished. They would no doubt have interrogated Gala about her domestic situation, and it would have been difficult for her to camouflage the *ménage à trois* with Ernst.

If Eluard embarked on his flight to force Gala into breaking off with Ernst, the ruse certainly failed. Brazenly, she travelled with Ernst to Germany. It is as though she never let Eluard forget his own complicity in the sexual triangle and was not about to be pushed into the role of repentant adultress. Eluard's own 'idiot voyage', as he described it, made him miserable. Without Gala there beside him, all the sights of shining beaches and Buddhist temples left him empty. For the first few weeks, Eluard sulkily chose not to write to her, his only correspondence a few archly jovial postcards showing Tahitian maidens in grass skirts, which he sent to Breton and a few others.

Then he cracked, begging Gala to join him. She waited several weeks before answering his pleas. There was no rush, no sense of panic. One has the impression that not for a minute did she ever take seriously Eluard's threat to 'disappear for ever'.

Eluard's father was less sure; he was willing to forgive his son just as long as he returned from the orient. It was decided that Gala should go to fetch him, leaving Cécile with her grandparents. Monsieur Grindel paid not only for Gala's trip around the world but also for Ernst, who travelled on a forged French passport with the name Gondolier. Ernst, in an autobiography as slapdash as some of his collages, takes credit for patching up Eluard's poor relations with his father. According to Ernst, he, not Gala, was entrusted with a message from Eluard's father urging him to come home, and promising not to be so dismissive of his son's artistic inclination. However, it seems odd that Monsieur Grindel would have chosen Ernst rather than his own daughter-in-law to be the bearer of reconciliation. Most likely, the prospect of a free trip around the world with Gala was too much to pass up, and Ernst may have convinced Monsieur Grindel that Eluard could be coaxed back only if he, as his best friend, threw his weight behind Gala's pleas.

Ernst seems to have lingered along the journey, letting Gala arrive in Saigon several days ahead of him, which seems odd if he were the genuine peacemaker. Eluard telegrammed his parents on Gala's arrival, 12 August. One can read a sort of apology in his short message: 'I've always loved you.'

It is not known whether Gala and Ernst were quarrelling or had simply decided that Gala would be more likely to persuade Eluard by herself. Whatever the reason, the three-way affair shattered in Saigon. Eluard and Gala rejoined; Ernst wandered around Asia afterwards without them. The charitable explanation is that Gala may have decided she valued her marriage more than a frivolous affair with Ernst. Another version, put forward by Ernst's acquaintances, was that the fickle German had grown tired of Gala and wanted to end it. Throughout his life, Ernst had a tendency to fall in love with women for a short, intense period and then drop them. He may have been only too happy to rid himself of Gala, especially with the bonus of a round-trip ticket to the orient.

That is the more credible explanation. A significant and cruel trait emerges in Gala. When her sexual advances were spurned – and this was to happen many times in her middle and old age while trying to seduce younger men – Gala would turn enormously vengeful. Her rage was unremitting and it clearly became so with Ernst. It seems likely that Gala, lured into infidelity by Eluard, decided that she enjoyed making love to more than one man. The problem was that Ernst no longer enjoyed being that other man.

Eluard and Gala sailed back full steam to Marseille, making only brief stopovers in Ceylon and India. They arrived home just one month after their Saigon rendezvous. When Ernst straggled back, laden with souvenirs and a drive to apply the primitive dynamism he had observed in Oceanic culture to his own art, he found the door at Eaubonne closed to him.

Gala portrayed the break-up as her doing, but perhaps she was too vulnerable to admit otherwise. Later, she was to remark callously: 'See, didn't I do well to spurn Ernst? He won't amount to much, while Dalí, after I got my hands on him – what a success!'

5

The Exquisite Corpse

Gala's feud with Ernst turned nastier. After leaving Eaubonne, Ernst fell in love with an ethereal young Frenchwoman, Marie-Berthe Aurèche. Gala, it seems, still occasionally felt proprietorial pangs towards him which made his new lover jealous. Although Marie-Berthe did not confront Gala face to face – few did – a conflict eventually took place.

It happened at an intimate party given by Breton in his flat, which visitors likened to an eclectic museum, filled with Picassos, de Chiricos, Duchamps, voodoo dolls and primitive African art. Marie-Berthe was there with Ernst. Eluard went alone, since Gala had returned to the Soviet Union, her first trip back since before the Revolution. Breton liked to dominate the talk, often turning parties into lectures or heated debates on topics as disparate as disbanding the army or the benefits of hysteria.

One surrealist, André Thirion, remembers that at these gatherings Eluard tended to be reticent. 'He spoke seldom but was articulate. His manner was a bit condescending.' On this occasion, his aloofness was shattered when Marie-Berthe suddenly turned to him and began crudely insulting Gala. Ernst intervened, trying at first to defend Gala. He told Marie-Berthe, his bride-to-be, that she was not 'in the same class as Gala'. As the ferocity of Eluard's retaliation against Marie-Berthe intensified, however, Ernst had no choice but to switch alliances.

A brawl erupted. Both men soon forgot about Marie-Berthe altogether and traded curses. Eluard called Ernst a 'dirty liar', and demanded an apology. It seems that the pent-up frustrations, the jealousies over Gala, the abortive trip to the orient and the hidden grievances of their close relationship all finally boiled over. Ernst swung first, punching Eluard so hard in the eye that he was temporarily blinded. Eluard flailed wildly, missing Ernst every time: he was humiliated. The other guests grabbed the two men, bringing an end to this 'confusing and regrettable scene', as Breton described it.

Eluard retreated to Eaubonne, where he remained for eight days until his eye healed. He contemplated shooting Ernst but rejected the idea 'out of love for Gala'. One senses from a tense, emotional letter he sent to Gala in Russia that her break with Ernst had not been a clean one. He pleaded with her not to write to Ernst: 'Don't betray me – otherwise,' he finished, 'I won't be able to live any more.' He was desperate for reassurance that Gala had not forsaken him. He promised to be faithful and to make love 'marvellously' the minute she came back to Paris.

Gala left Russia after five days, without even seeing her family. She only reached as far as Moscow before turning around in disgust at the changes in Russia since the tsar's overthrow. Her abrupt departure came as a blow to the Diakonovs, for they had suffered much hardship during the Revolution and Gala's letters were often the only source of diversion. 'She found the police surveillance unbearable,' said her sister Lidia. 'Gala had a permit to stay for three weeks but she couldn't even stand it for a week.'

This seems a feeble excuse. Through her marriage into Eluard's family, Gala was well-off, certainly more comfortable than her family in Kazan; it therefore seems strange that she did not visit or bring them any packages of food or goods that they might have lacked since the Revolution. Time after time, Gala was to exhibit an obliviousness to the misery of her family and friends. It could have been out of spite, revenge for their little betrayals and disappointments; or it is equally possible that Gala's state of well-being was so fragile, so precarious, that she could only sustain herself by blotting out the misfortunes of those near to her. Later, after Dalí became rich, Gala was to be far more generous to strangers than to her relatives.

By early 1927, surrealism was in full swing and Breton was its undisputed, autocratic leader. As his lieutenants he had a theor-etician, Louis Aragon, and a poet, Paul Eluard. From Breton's art-deco 'laboratory' with its porthole windows at 42 rue de la Fontaine, they published *La Révolution surréaliste*. Its cover was designed so that it could easily be mistaken for an obscure scien-tific journal. Its contents, however, were nothing short of incendiary. The triumvirate challenged that which was most sacred in France: the Pope (a 'dog' and a 'merchant of souls') and *la République* itself. It was not a revolution made in literary salons but a guerrilla movement using shock tactics. Benjamin Péret, for one, prowled Paris looking for priests to insult loudly.

Not surprisingly, the surrealists had many enemies. Art and literature critics on the big newspapers crusaded against them, and often gangs of patriotic thugs – the Camelots du Roi and the Jeunesses Patriotiques – would invade the cafés frequented by the surrealists and beat them with wooden clubs.

The preferred haunt of the surrealists was a café only a few steps away from Breton's flat – and an even shorter distance from the Moulin Rouge nightclub. The Café Cyrano in the Place Blanche was working class, packed with butchers and florists from the nearby market on the rue Tholoze and the prostitutes of Pigalle. Gala was often there along with Eluard listening to Breton holding court. She often struck people as being bored and aloof during these sessions. Breton was not to everyone's taste. Tyrannical to the point of absurdity, he insisted that all good surrealists drink Pernod, because it was not 'bourgeois'. Breton, a student of alchemy, also found a portent in how the anise spirit, when mixed with water, transformed into a milky substance. Aragon – who was later banned from the group – was the only one to resist and drink vermouth. Often Breton read aloud: his selections ranged from attacks on the surrealists in *Le Figaro* to fragments from a manifesto entitled *Judas, The Surrealist Vampire*, written by an addled ex-Jesuit.

Breton would invite debate like a schoolmaster. Those who listened raptly included some of the most influential artists in Europe at the time. The regulars in 1927 were the painters Yves Tanguy, André Masson, Max Ernst, Marcel Duchamp and Man Ray, and also such writers as René Crevel. René Char, Jacques Prévert and Benjamin Péret. Occasional visitors included René Magritte, Joan Mirò, Hans Arp and the dramatist Antonin Artaud.

Gala, as André Thirion remembers, was always elegantly dressed and haughty at these gatherings. 'Gala knew what she wanted, the pleasures of the heart and the senses, money and the companionship of genius. She wasn't interested in politics or philosophy. She judged people by their efficiency in the real world and eliminated those who were mediocre.' Yet, added

Thirion with apparent perplexity: 'She could inspire the passions and exalt the creative forces of men as diverse as Ernst, Dalí and Eluard.' It was said, apocryphally, perhaps, that whenever a surrealist created a good work of art his companions would remark: 'Ah, well, he was in love with Gala, then.'

Breton was also a prude and, as with drink, he imposed himself on the private lives of his surrealist subjects. He found homosexuals aberrant and believed that the 'passion' of surrealism could only be reached through the union of a man and a woman, a union based on fidelity. At the time, Gala's affair with Ernst was an open secret, and Breton would have found out. Gala's reaction was to seek the company of other outcasts. Her closest friend, her only confidant, was René Crevel, a homosexual writer and poet. Eluard, too, ran into trouble for his extramarital frivolities, and Breton chastised him for his 'shallow' licentiousness. This licentiousness was, in part, a sham: according to Thirion, 'Eluard loved libertinage, bordellos and orgies more as a spectator and dilettante than as a participant.'

Women played a more active role in surrealism than in any artistic movement that preceeded it. They were no longer mere muses or supportive mother figures. Meret Oppenheim was probably the most original, with her fur-lined teacups and her enigmatic sculptures, but the painters Léonor Fini and Valentine Hugo were also treated as equals by the surrealist men. Simone and Elsa, the wives of Breton and Aragon, were both intellectuals who commanded as much respect in surrealist debates as did their husbands. Gala's contributions to the surrealist body of work were limited to a few drawings in the Exquisite Corpse game, an amusement in which a paper would be folded over and each participant would draw something – anything – without knowing what the others had done. Gala often drew breasts covered with antennae-like feelers.

It seemed a childish amusement, a sort of cerebral charade, but according to Breton, 'what excited us . . . was the assurance that, for better or worse, they bore the mark of something which could not be created by one brain alone.' It was this spirit of collectivity which brought the surrealist women into their own. Whitney Chadwick, in her book *The Muses of Surrealism*, claims that Breton, Eluard and the rest drew heavily on the symbolist literature of the turn of the century for their interpretation of women. The surrealists, according to Chadwick, wanted their women to be 'beautiful, independent and creative', a fusion between an ethereal, inspirational being and an active, down-to-earth woman who could bake surrealist objects out of marzipan, be uninhibited in bed and join in the great adventure. Gala could not cook (her dishes, Dalí once complained, all tasted like his handkerchief), but she was a consummate surrealist woman at everything else. Her art lay in her sensitivity; whether with Eluard, Ernst or Dali, she had an unerring instinct for what an artist was trying to accomplish. Eluard, who always showed Gala his poems, said: 'Her compliments are the only ones that matter.'

Early on, in 1922, Ernst also honoured his debt to Gala's influence by painting her in the corner of a group portrait, *At the Rendezvous of Friends*. Gala is the only woman. She stands apart from Eluard, next to a bust of Giorgio de Chirico and Robert Desnos, the writer. Her neck is long and milky white; she seems imbued with all the sensuality and composure of a cat. Her eyebrows are arched over big dark eyes, and she manages to signal her attractiveness and independence at the same time. Gala's features had changed since the Swiss sanatorium photographs. The chubbiness of her face had receded, revealing Slavic cheekbones. She had become as sleek as a Parisian model and accentuated her feline litheness by wearing the long, muted-coloured gowns popular at the time. Sensitive about her short height (she barely cleared five feet), Gala wore a hat to gain a few extra inches.

Perhaps the aloofness that Thirion noted of Gala at the surrealist soirées was only a mask for her insecurity. She was harshly self-critical. By her own exacting standards, she lacked any talent for writing or painting and she was as hard on other aspiring artists as she was on herself. Her contributions to the Exquisite Corpse game were timid drawings, revealing nothing of herself or her inner fantasies. It is as if she was too intimidated by the flair of the other players to dare express herself. Alone with an artist, though, Gala easily proved an equal. One may imagine the scene after the Café Cyrano crowd had drifted apart and Breton had led the Eluards and a few of their favoured acolytes off to a working men's café for dinner: only then, when Gala could turn her incisive intelligence on one individual, did she enter into her element. Her criticism could be devastating, her praise lucid and from the heart.

One artist who met Gala at this time was Pablo Picasso. Though he was not a surrealist, his originality was recognised early on by Eluard and Breton, who dedicated a special edition of *Littér-ature* to him, and Eluard and Picasso became close friends. Some say that Gala had an affair with Picasso, but there is no evidence for this. However, in a rare display of magnanimity, Picasso, who was as noted for his monetary meanness as he was for his womanising, once let Gala have her pick of any painting in his studio. Gala was canny enough to have understood Picasso's mean streak and, to the artist's great relief, she marched straight to the smallest canvas and said, 'This is the one I want.' They remained friends long after.

By 1929 the time was ripe for a new romance. Gala's long and painful love affair with Ernst, even after its ending, had cast a shadow over her marriage with Eluard. The euphoria of their first years, the commitment Gala made to Eluard, that desire which drove her across Russia to Paris in the middle of a war – all seemed to have evaporated. Gala and Eluard drew apart from each other. Jealousy, unspoken treacheries, games of who could inflict more pain on the other in the name of surrealist passion had taken their toll. The Gala that emerges seems cynical and hard, but stronger too. She found she was desirable. She learned that the source of her individuality did not spring from Eluard. She mattered not because she was the pretty little wife of a poet but because she was Gala, part groupie, part icon. But there was a void in her life. She needed to pour her energy into someone else's creativity. She needed to fall intensely in love again, to nurture and protect the artistry of another person, to make that artistry her own.

That person was Salvador Dalí. Her relationship with Dalí was to last over fifty years. Later they became rich, leading the most extravagant life of any artist and his woman this century – but it was not without sacrifice. Gala would first suffer poverty, attend to the whims and nightmares of a genius, and help shape his morbid vision.

6

Seducing The Executioner

In his autobiography, Dalí embarks on a curious detour during the story of how Gala seduced him. The Cadaqués walks at sunset, their courtship punctuated by Dalí's uncontrollable laughter, the images of Gala's lithe body are all abandoned in his narrative, while he recounts a Catalonian folk-tale of an evil king. Dalí readily identifies with the tyrant. As the story goes, every morning three girls would be escorted into the castle gardens where, from a secluded balcony, the king would choose the most beautiful and have her brought to his bedchamber that evening. The naked king would command the girl to lie beside him, as still as death. The king never touched her until dawn. Then the king arose and beheaded the girl with his sword.

The fate of these maidens was known throughout the kingdom, and one day the king selected a girl whose intelligence matched her astonishing beauty. She smuggled a wax dummy with a sugar nose into the king's chamber, and while the monarch slept she slid the dummy in beside him and hid. In the morning, when the king cut off the dummy's head, the sugar nose flew right into his mouth. Tasting the sweetness, the king was sorry he had killed her. At that moment, the girl appeared from under the bed and the king was somehow cured of his 'criminal aberration'.

Dalí's own interpretation of this tale – that the king is a necrophiliàc – is deliberately elusive and leaves the reader wondering why he has included it in such a crucial part of his story. A simpler answer exists: both Dalí and the king are terrified of their own sexuality. The difference is that the king finds it easier to slay the object of his desire than his own fears.

By his own admission, when he met Gala Dalí was a twenty-four-year-old virgin. An explanation is given by his cousin,

Gonzalo Serraclara, who said that Dalí, as an impressionable young teenager, found a medical textbook of sexual diseases that his father had left on the piano. The book was filled with photographs and drawings of men and women ravaged by every imaginable form of gonorrhoea and syphilis. This dread surfaces in several paintings: in one, a boy in a sailor-suit stands on a beach before a giant elongated woman who is decomposing. At an early age, sex was equated with the worst kind of death. The hideous images of the medical textbook fused, during Dalí's adolescence, with a family catastrophe. Dalí's mother died after a lingering illness, and almost immediately after his mother was buried his father married the sister of Dalí's mother who had been living with them for several years. Some of the artist's biographers have speculated that Dalí's father may have been having an affair with her while his wife was still living, and this may have added to the boy's sexual confusion. Dalí's natural rebelliousness erupted into all-out war with his father. There were other disquieting reasons for his terror. Salvador was named after an older brother, 'a perfect angel', who had died as a baby, and the artist was forever escaping this macabre shadow.

Fear mixed with Dalí's delirious attachment to Gala. 'I was convinced that she was going to do me harm,' he writes. If one can believe Dalí's somewhat fantastical autobiography, one afternoon with Gala he came close to copying the homicidal king.

After Eluard withdrew to Paris, Dalí coaxed her into walking with him out to Cape Creus, a desolate point about seven kilometres beyond the Cadaqués cemetery. Dalí led her along the old fishermen's path that rose up a ridge past the cemetery to a sheltered bay on the other side called Port Lligat. There was a cluster of stone huts where the fishermen stored their nets and drank when the Tramontana blew too strong. A few years later, when Dalí was banished from his father's house – partly because of Gala – the couple would take refuge in one of these huts.

One can imagine Dalí's impatience as he pulled Gala along over charred, volcanic land that seemed to be still smouldering. He was taking her to see the Eagle, a stone formation of red and white quartz perched on a dark sea cliff. At Cape Creus one has the impression that the clash and coupling of continents has spawned a zoo of sinister rock animals. They are as spiny as sea predators and shine, malformed, with a dark unnatural light. It is as if the creation continues, terrible and invisible, at the slow pace of stone. Star-lichens are the only plants that survive, vivid as wounds.

Gala and Dalí entered this rock garden like two trespassers. The atmosphere was menacing, the stones blade-sharp. They climbed. Gala liked wearing shorts, and Dalí was animally attentive to her 'delicate buttocks'. 'I insisted pitilessly on Gala's climbing to the top of all the most dangerous summits, which reached great heights,' Dalí writes. 'These ascents involved obvious criminal intentions on my part.' He took her to the height of the Eagle. The granite cliff fell away sharply below them, studded around its blue edges with sea urchins. Dalí rolled a large rock over the cliff, which clattered deep into the water with a resounding splash. He enjoyed the effect, rolling another and another. Soon he was hurling down boulders, glaring at Gala. 'She . . . had come to destroy and annihilate my solitude, and I began to overwhelm her with absolutely unjust reproaches: she prevented me from working, she insinuated herself surreptitiously into my brain, she "depersonalised" me.'

If Dalí's tale is true – and one should be sceptical – he would like us to believe that he intended to murder her, much as the Catalonian king would have done. He would also like us to believe that Gala was aware of this danger. She vomited and was seized with convulsions – so he says – and yet she stayed with him. He does not say this, but it seems that Gala was weighing which force was stronger in Dalí: the wish to make love to her or the longing to murder her because he could not.

Even with Eluard gone, they were not entirely free. Gala needed to care for the sick Cécile, though her main preoccupation was undoubtedly Dalí. The Dalí household contained a shrine of the Virgin holding a twig of red coral; the poet, Federico García Lorca, had placed the coral in the Virgin's hands. The treatment that Dalí's father and younger sister accorded the painter was, in its way, just as reverential – and protective.

The hours that Gala would spend in Dalí's small grey studio in the beach house concerned them. They knew Gala was married, had a child whom she seemed to be neglecting and a husband who had left without her. It was also apparent that Salvador was infatuated with this imperious Russian woman. Dalí's family began fearing for him. The sister, Ana Maria, was extremely wary of Gala. After their father remarried, Dalí had made his sister the feminine figure of his life, painting her portrait

49

many times and letting her into his secret world. Now Ana Maria sensed that Gala was a threat. She wrote of Gala's arrival as though she were the snake slithering into the Garden of Eden: 'The mica of the rocks . . . the shine of the sun on the sea, the silver of the olive leaves all trembled with terror when those strange people [the Parisian set] . . . gazed at them with their bloodshot eyes.' She also blamed Gala and the other foreigners for Dalí's hysteria and the nightmarish forms sprouting from his canvases. Ana Maria believed these strange people exhibited a 'fanatic' haste in destroying the bounds of 'morality and family'. Ana Maria's rancour towards Gala never subsided, even after half a century.

Camille Goëmans and his wife lingered in Cadaqués, as did Buñuel, who was having little success persuading Dalí to co-write the screenplay of his new film, *L'Age d'or*. Gala was to blame for this, according to Buñuel, who maintained that she had taken offence at a remark he had made about thin women's thighs. 'I found myself saying [to Gala] that what repelled me more than anything else in the female anatomy was when a woman had a large space between her thighs. The next day we went out swimming, and, to my embarrassment, I saw that Gala had just this unfortunate physical attribute.'

Buñuel described Dalí's transformation that summer in his autobiography, *My Last Breath*. 'All he could talk about was Gala; he echoed every word she uttered.' Moreover, she criticised every word that Buñuel uttered.

Once, during a picnic, Buñuel rebelled most violently against Gala's stinging remarks. He hurled her down and began squeezing her neck with his hands. Buñuel had the strength of a prizefighter. 'Dalí fell to his knees and begged me to stop; I was in a blind rage, but I knew I wasn't going to kill her. Strange as it may seem, all I wanted was to see the tip of her tongue between her teeth.'

Cécile was on the beach with Gala at the time. 'Buñuel was a huge man with bulging eyes, and he was choking my mother. I was terrified.' Cécile cried and cried. Although Cécile was eleven, she says that her only memory of Cadaqués was of this violent incident. Perhaps her response to the undercurrent of tension between her parents was to erase all other discomforting recollections of the trip.

After losing his temper with Gala, Buñuel thought it wise to retreat from Cadaqués. The Goëmanses departed too, taking Gala and Cécile's letters back to Paris for Eluard. Gala needed Eluard to send her money, which he did, with a pathetic note: 'I'm so very, *very happy* that you have good memories of my being with you in Cadaqués.'

Left alone, with Cécile in her hotel room, Gala and Dalí continued their courtship, feverish and chaste. Dalí still had not dared kiss her. Gala could have tried to seduce him, but what would have happened? If Dalí was as murderously confused as he claims in his autobiography, her forwardness could have provoked a brutal response; or, more likely, at her first caress, Dalí would have simply fled to his studio and resumed painting excrement. Instead, Gala chose to play the victim. She dressed in white and was as passive as the virgins who lay stone-still beside Dalí's demented king.

As Dalí explains it, Gala allowed his passion – and courage – to ripen like the sweet grapes on the Cadaqués vines that September. The Tramontana wind blew off the Pyrenees with a relentlessness that, according to the Catalonians, drives some people mad. Dalí and Gala sheltered among the rocks, facing the turbulent sea. Dalí believed that his own 'physical state' had begun to erode Gala's calm. His repression and anxiety, in other words, were shared. Lately, on their walks, the tension had silenced conversation completely.

'What do you want me to do to you?' Dalí asked finally.

Gala wept. According to Dalí, 'She made several attempts to speak, and finally she shook her head abruptly, while tears flowed down her cheeks. I kept insisting. She replied: "If you won't do it, you promise not to tell anyone?"'

Dalí for the first time, kissed her on the mouth, awakening his 'tyrannised' erotic desires. He seized Gala's hair and pulled her head back.

'Now,' commanded Dalí, 'tell me what you want me to do to you! But tell me slowly, looking me in the eye, with the crudest, the most ferociously erotic words that can make us both feel the greatest shame!'

Even Dalí was shocked by Gala's response. With a calm determination, she replied: 'I want you to kill me!'

But was this startling, theatrical reply true? We have only Dalí's account of this scene, and Dalí is often a mischievous liar, a self-fabulist. It makes for good drama, and Gala was never one to pinprick Dalí's epic version of their love. That was how his paintings were sold, his artistic reputation inflated.

On the other hand, it could be true. Gala could have said, 'Kill me.' Dalí was an extraordinary man who elicited extraordinary responses from people. That day there were no witnesses, no fishermen, no jealous sister spying on them from behind a rock who would tell otherwise. Let us assume that there are people who romance in this way, with an invitation to murder. Did Gala really mean it? Was she subject to a kind of mercurial hollowness? A moralist would say so, and attribute it to the greed and wantonness from which she would desire escape, punishment. Gala told Dalí that she wanted to experience death 'cleanly' and so swiftly there would be no time for fear. Dalí wrote: 'Gala had begun to explain to me minutely the reasons for her wish and it suddenly occurred to me that she, too, had an inner world of desires and frustrations, and moved with a rhythm of her own between poles of lucidity and madness.'

Seldom, however, will a depressive choose another human for a suicide weapon. People are notoriously unreliable in such matters. The most likely explanation is that Gala had no death wish; it was a shrewd psychological move. She had tremendous vitality and perseverance, and her intuition about other people was uncanny. It was a gift she would exploit, and it is possible that she did so with Dalí, gambling that once she exposed his homicidal desire, and gave him the opportunity to act upon it, he wouldn't.

With the meticulousness of 'a mistress of the house giving orders for the laying of the table', Gala outlined specific instructions for how the deed should be done so that Dalí would not be blamed for the crime. Poison was discarded as too painful, pulling the trigger of a revolver too complicated for Dalí. But would he agree to be her executioner?

Dalí seized her in his arms and solemnly said: 'YES!'

But, of course, he didn't. Instead, Dalí hoisted Gala's loose white skirt and, doing untold damage to his knees on the fakir's bed of sharp rocks, tried to make love to her. In his autobiography Dalí is unusually coy about the episode, but in another, novelistic memoir, *The Unspeakable Confessions of Salvador Dalí*, he is rather more explicit: 'My limbs no longer belonged to me, an unbelievable strength had possession of me. I felt myself a man, freed from my terrors and my impotence. By her, I was henceforth gifted with the telluric vertical forces such as allow a man to penetrate a woman.'

Something happened there on the rocks, while the maddening wind blew. It will never be known whether Gala really asked Dalí to kill her; but the evidence suggests that, if not in that way, then in another, Gala was able to cure Dalí. His laughing fits and his hysteria ceased. In return, Dalí was able to give Gala wealth and, through his devotion and genius, he helped her reach a deeper understanding of herself. The drift of her days with Eluard had ended, and she and Dalí embarked on a strange and fruitful conspiracy.

However, there was one terrible flaw in their relationship. That September day was the first time that Dalí had tried sexual intercourse. It may also have been the last time. Dalí could give Gala much, but he was incapable of sexual loving. He was a voyeur who could reach climax only through masturbation.

7

Blood Sweeter Than Honey

The Hotel Terrasse seemed to fit Eluard's melancholic mood, for the windows of his room opened on to Montmartre cemetery. It was September, 1929. For three weeks Gala had remained behind in Cadaqués with Dalí. She had written once asking Eluard to send her face rouge, but he had refused. His tolerance was beginning to fray. Eluard promised to make her 'elegant and happy' – but only when she returned to Paris. The weather in Paris was unseasonably hot for September, and he found it difficult to concentrate on any serious writing.

Eluard's frustration over Gala's absence was heightened by the fact that he had committed himself to buying an expensive flat on the rue Becquerel, a short descent down a stone stairway from the Sacré-Cœur church. The flat was modern and commanded one of the grandest views of Paris. Eluard had done it all for Gála. She had complained of feeling trapped at their current house in the suburb of Eaubonne. Raising chickens no longer held much fascination for her. Nor did motherhood: increasingly, Gala was relinquishing care of Cécile to Eluard's mother and going off her on independent travels, in Switzerland and on the Côte d'Azur. What Eluard hoped was that the flat might help to halt Gala's drifting and reunite them as a family. But Dalí was different from all her past flings.

Eluard had gone to great lengths to please Gala with the flat. The death of his father in 1927 had left him with a rich inheritance but also with a sizeable amount of guilt. Eluard's abrupt trip to the orient had shocked the old man badly; Eluard never forgave himself for this, even though he was now finally freed from a business career. A good portion of his inheritance was spent on the flat; he had also sold off several paintings by Picasso and de Chirico. When the heat grew too oppressive for writing, Eluard would wander up Montmartre and view the flat. An oval room, which rang with the bells of Sacré-Cœur, was set aside for Gala. He had bought her a mirrored vanity table, art deco and so new it smelled of varnish. He had written a line of poetry in large script across the centre mirror:

With one caress, I can make you shine your brightest.

Having a seamstress for a mother had given Eluard an impeccable sense of fashion. As a surprise, he had filled Gala's wardrobes with new dresses from the most artful couturiers. The motion of the closet doors sliding open swirled the brilliant silk gowns inside like tropical fish in an aquarium.

Eluard missed her terribly. 'Last night,' he wrote, 'I had the most magnificent masturbation thinking of you, imagining you loving and unleashed as you have taught me to see you.'

The flat was only a short walk from the surrealist gathering at the Café Cyrano in the Place Blanche. Eluard descended the market street of Tholoze, past stalls selling fish, pots and pans, bread and the last of the summer roses. There was no escaping Dalí. Outside the cinema Studio 28, workmen on ladders were removing *The Sign of Zorro* from the façade and putting in its place *Un Chien Andalou*. It was the film's first public showing, though it had been screened before, privately, to a select group of artists and artistocrats, Picasso and Le Corbusier were among them. During that exclusive showing, Buñuel had faced the crowd alone – and expected the worst. He had filled his pockets with stones to hurl at the audience in case they turned violent. However, *Un Chien Andalou* had been a success, and Buñuel had discreetly emptied the stones from his pockets behind the screen. Dalí had been painting in Cadaqués and had not bothered to attend the private première.

Eluard had another reminder of Dalí – and the calamitous holiday in Cadaqués. Coincidentally, Buñuel was also staying in the Hotel Terrasse. He had returned to Paris empty-handed from Cadaqués. When Eluard pressed him for details of Cécile and Gala, Buñuel was curiously evasive. Later, Eluard was to discover that Buñuel had tried to strangle Gala and had left Cadaqués rather hastily afterwards, without attempting to pin down Dalí for a screenplay to *L'Age d'or*.

The excuse Gala gave for not returning to Cadaqués sooner

was Cécile's poor health. However, that excuse seemed thin when she wrote to Eluard informing him that, instead of boarding the first train to Paris after Cécile's recovery, she wished to spend time in Barcelona with Dalí. Eluard's irritation wore through, as he counselled her against this 'fatiguing' side-trip, and his sigh is almost audible in his letter: 'Very well, my pretty dear. [I know] you'll do what you want.' She did.

It was near the end of September when Gala and Cécile returned at last. Gala had brought Dalí's painting, *Le Jeu Lugubre* (*The Lugubrious Game*, titled by Eluard), which was to hang in the Galerie Goëmans that November. She also carried a suitcase full of notes and jottings. These, she explained enthusiastically, were Dalí's and would establish that he was not only a gifted painter but also a first-rate theoretician. Dalí would be arriving in Paris that November. The exhibition at the Galerie Goëmans was Dalí's first in Paris. The invitations – discreet cards, printed in red and black, – had already been sent out. Gala extolled Dalí's talents whenever she was with the surrealists.

Breton was curious, anxious even, to recruit Dalí. Surrealism seemed to be running short of ideas. Breton's inquisitorial style had driven away some of its ablest practitioners. Earlier that year a dozen of Breton's followers had defected, including André Masson, Robert Desnos and André Thirion, who once wrote that Breton's genius lay 'in creating a high temperature of revelation by stage-managing tests and clashes for better or worse'. There was also a vengeful side to Breton – one he would eventually inflict on Dalí and Gala. Breton's sting was felt by the twelve defectors, who had decided that the French Communist Party was a more realistic instrument of change than surrealism. Around the time that Leon Trotsky was banished from the Kremlin, posters began to appear in all the cafés patronised by the defectors announcing a symposium on the issue. The identity of the symposium's sponsor was a mystery, but Trotsky's expulsion was a topic that had split the French Communist Party and excited keen debate. The twelve surrealist defectors took the bait. They were outraged to discover that the mystery organiser was Breton. When Breton spoke from the podium, the subject of Trotsky was soon abandoned and Breton gleefully launched into an attack on every defector in the audience.

Under Breton's dogmatism, surrealism meandered. The avenues of automatic writing had come to a dead-end, and the shock tactics of the surrealist armoury were beginning to seem humdrum. Gala, using ideas she had been able to decipher from conversations with Dalí and from his voluminous notes, tried to convince Breton that Dalí had enough originality to fill the vacuum left by the surrealist renegades. As best she could, Gala tried to explain Dalí's theory of art. Dalí called it his theory of paranoiac-critical activity. In short, Dalí believed that the delirium of dream fragments could be assembled in such a way as to be understood the very instant a viewer cast his eye on the canvas. But was it surrealist? As Gala explained it, yes, the theory was. Dalí used classical technique but did so to unveil the irrational, the 'omnipotence of dreams'.

Gala's championing of Dalí was remarkable considering that not once had he bothered to write to her after she left Cadaqués.

The flat on the rue Becquerel was nearly finished. All it needed was a coat of paint and for the delivery men to bring the modern furniture that Eluard had commissioned from a designer friend. Cécile was probably sent off to Eluard's mother-in-law at Montlignon, leaving Gala and Eluard alone together after so many weeks apart. They stayed at the Hotel Terrasse, but when Gala heard that Buñuel was also residing there she panicked. Buñuel was a madman, she insisted, who would try to kill her again. Gala described the strangling on the beach so vividly that Eluard immediately went out and purchased a pearl-handled revolver. According to Buñuel, Eluard never left the hotel room without his little gun.

At this stage Gala gave no indication that she would be abandoning Eluard for Dalí. Perhaps she wasn't sure herself. Two months still remained before Dalí was due to arrive, and she had no assurance, no guarantee, that his passion for her would endure such a long absence. There was even some likelihood that Dalí's flightiness and fears of such things as telephones and buying train tickets would prevent him from coming to Paris. Perhaps Gala's evangelical belief in his artistry was enough to blind her to such personal defects.

With the exhibition due to open on 20 November, Dalí was still painting feverishly and delayed his arrival in Paris as long as possible. Goëmans was even more worried than Gala: the gallery owner had only a pair of Dalís to hang on his walls. It was just a few days before the exhibition that Dalí disembarked at the Gare du Nord with several paintings, including *The Great*

Masturbator. Dalí was nervous about Gala and the success of his forthcoming exhibition. The Métro terrified him, so he ordered a taxi driver to take him to the finest florist in the city. In his broken French, Dalí mistakenly ordered 3000 roses for Gala, but this extravagance was too much, even for him. He bought several dozen, and staggered out of the florist's under his burden of thorns, suitcase and paintings. He did not go straight to Gala, claiming that he wanted to prolong the expectation of ecstasy, but more likely he was too stricken by anxiety to see her at once.

Fortifying himself with a few Pernods along the way, Dalí walked to the Galerie Goëmans, on a crooked street leading through the Left Bank to the river Seine. By an odd coincidence, Eluard happened to be at the gallery when Dalí lurched in with his roses and paintings. One of the canvases that Dalí uncrated was his portrait of Eluard.

In his autobiography Dalí does not comment on Eluard's reaction at seeing him, his wife's new lover. One imagines that Eluard retained his veneer of politeness. According to Dalí, Eluard 'told me that Gala was very much surprised that I had not paid her a visit, nor even let her know when I would meet her. This astonished me greatly, for I had a vague intention of drifting along for several days in this state of waiting, which appeared to me filled with all manner of delights.' If this is true, one wonders why Dalí had bought the roses.

That same evening, Dalí paid a call on Gala, climbing the spiral of narrow alleys up to the Sacré-Cœur. He passed a small vineyard, the only one in Paris, which is said to yield a bitter wine. The rue Becquerel twisted, vine-like, into the shadows of the stone basilica. In the autumn twilight, old men drank wine and played boules on a sandy pitch beside the Eluards' apartment building. Dalí's roses had all withered.

Gala did not hide her anger with Dalí. It had been impossible for her not to read from Dalí's absolute silence that he had lost interest. Dalí said that Gala's wrath lasted 'for only a moment'. Other guests were there, and drinks flowed. Dalí claims he was able to persuade all assembled that he was not 'an utter cretin'.

That evening, after the Russian vodka was drained and all the guests had gone, did Gala walk out on Eluard? Did she move Dalí immediately into her bedroom? At times she could be brutally direct. Gala probably stayed at home, washed up the dirty plates and glasses, and gave the clear impression, to Eluard, at least, that no amorous affair of hers would ever shake the spiritual bedrock of their marriage. It was not true, but Gala did not discourage Eluard from thinking so. Her short-range strategy was one she had perfected several years earlier with Max Ernst: that is, to keep both husband and lover dangling.

Her qualms at ditching Eluard and Cécile were not necessarily moral ones. Money mattered to her a great deal. Since childhood, when her family was left in poverty by her gold-prospecting father, Gala had been prey to a panicky avarice, and she abhorred having to withdraw money from a bank account. Although she and Dalí were eventually to become millionaires, at that point Dalí barely eked out an existence. Eluard had received a fair inheritance from his father, while Dalí survived on a small allowance from his father and an even smaller advance from Goëmans.

Sex also mattered to Gala, and Dalí, despite his passion, was a woeful lover. By his own admission, Dalí was fixated on masturbation and would suffer sexual contact with only the greatest anxiety. His interest in the female anatomy seemed to centre exclusively on the buttocks. Eluard, at least in his letters, emerges as an able and inventive lover.

It is also possible that Gala held on to Eluard because she never stopped loving him. She hoarded his letters. Jean-Claude Carrière, the noted screenwriter and author of the foreword to Eluard's *Letters to Gala*, said: 'Gala survived Eluard for 30 years. During those 30 years she saved his correspondence, even the telegrams and postcards – she who professed to be an enemy of all [sentimental] memories. Did she reread these letters? One doesn't know. Maybe she forgot about them.'

However much Gala loved Eluard she loved Dalí more, incandescently. She was also convinced that Dalí was a genius. Part of this was good public relations but it also happened to be sincere. In letters to her sister she is just as reverential about Dalí's work as she would be to a rich client. Having Dalí embark on a new painting, one feels, was almost as all-consuming for her as it was for him. Dalí describes, with grateful astonishment, how he inspired 'a devoted and pressing fanaticism' in Gala.

Eluard was not the type of husband to brandish his pearl-handled revolver and order Dalí to stay away from his wife. Nor does Gala seem to have been the type of woman to be won back by such masculine posturing.

Dalí had scarcely hung up his new work in the art gallery

when he and Gala decided they could not bear their separation any longer. Just two days before the exhibition opened, his first in Paris, he and Gala fled on a 'honeymoon' to Barcelona and then further south to Sitges, a fishing village. Since Dalí had squandered his cheque from Goëmans, presumably Gala had no choice but to ask her husband for the 'honeymoon' funds – and presumably the long-suffering Eluard obliged.

Of this trip, Dalí wrote: 'I confess that during our voyage, Gala and I were so occupied by our two bodies that we hardly for a single moment thought about my exhibition, which I already looked upon as ours.' Even without his own presence there to dazzle the viewers, Dalí's show had been a success, and all the paintings were sold. Breton bought one, as did the Vicomte de Noailles and his wife, Marie-Laure, the rich patrons of surrealism.

Back in Paris, Eluard did not mope. René Char, a burly ex-rugby player turned surrealist, moved in with him at the rue Becquerel. The pretty brunette that Eluard hired as a maid turned out to be a prostitute who worked the boulevard de la Madeleine by night. According to Thirion, 'The maid finally quit rue Becquerel because the men took up too much of her time.'

Then Eluard found Nusch. She was a moon-eyed waif, a failed actress, whom he picked off the street. Thirion said: 'Nusch was dressed like the devil, without any shelter, money, dying of hunger and ready to take a client for warmth and to sleep under a roof. She falls passionately in love with him, and Eluard is very moved.' It seems Nusch was too grateful to challenge Eluard's persistent liaisons with Gala. Eluard would remain with Nusch until her death in 1946.

Dalí and Gala's idyll together in Sitges lasted through December. No letters from Eluard have survived from that period: either the letters were lost or Eluard maintained a huffy silence. It is just as likely, though, that he was too distracted by his housemaid and Nusch to bother.

Dalí was still wrestling with his growing emotional dependence on Gala. An inexhaustible worker, he began to panic over not having painted for nearly two and a half months. 'This can't last forever,' he finally told Gala. 'You know that I must live alone.' Dutifully, Gala returned from Sitges to Paris. However, Dalí did not intend this separation to last; he went home to Figueras to announce his love for Gala. His father, a stern notary, knew all about Gala from the previous summer. He knew that she was Russian, ten years older than his son, and already married with a daughter. He violently opposed his son's relationship with her and, according to Dalí, went so far as to accuse Gala of being a drug addict who had corrupted Dalí into becoming a narcotics trafficker. For the father, this alone, writes Dalí, 'would explain the unlikely sums of money I have been making'. The art dealer Goëmans had in fact given him a lucrative two-year-contract, which Dalí quickly squandered.

After stalking off from Figueras to the family's summer villa in Cadaqués, Dalí received a terrible letter from his father. The echoes of a frivolously provocative statement that he had made back in Paris – 'I spit on my mother's picture' – had reached home. This shock, together with his liaison, proved too much for the artist's father, who refused to forgive this sacrilege. Dalí was banished from the family, stripped of any inheritance and cursed by his father that he might die alone and poor among strangers. The father finally forgave his son, six years later. However, Dalí's sister, Ana Maria, was never so kind. For over thirty years Dalí and his sister never spoke, even though they both lived in Cadaqués, a town of no more than 2000 inhabitants. They spent much of their time dodging each other. Dalí's cousin, Gonzalo Serraclara, maintained that this rift between brother and sister was over Gala: 'Ana Maria hated her deeply. Dalí's father later got on well with Gala but Ana Maria did not. It was she who really made the reconciliation impossible.'

Dalí's advance from the dealer had run out. Cast out of his family, with no money and nowhere to stay, he returned to Paris, to Gala, having decided that he could no longer live without her.

Gala was in for a shock when he arrived. He had shaved himself bald in a sort of penance for disgracing his family. All of that lustrous black hair had been buried back on the beach at Cadaqués, together with the remains of a lunch of sea urchin. For Gala there was no question of Dalí's staying anywhere but with her at the rue Becquerel. She took him under her wing, fed him, probably lent him some of Eluard's money and salved his bruised ego. Gala was more convinced of his genius than Dalí himself.

Eluard's reaction to having a new houseguest was typically muted. He absented himself from the flat. Cécile was now living permanently with her grandmother. It was not the 'idiot voyage' of several years before but a strategic retreat. Judging from Eluard's letters to Gala during this period, he never abandoned hope that one day she would grow tired of Dalí and return to him.

Gala threw herself into the promotion of Dalí. Through her writer friend, René Crevel, she arranged an introduction with a rich young art collector, the Prince de Faucigny-Lucinge, who had brought one of Dalí's canvases at the Goëmans show. The prince belonged to one of France's oldest and most aristocratic families. Crevel, the prince, the timid Dalí and Gala all lunched at a restaurant near Montsouri park. The Prince de Faucigny-Lucinge was enthralled by Dalí – less so by Gala: 'She had enormous charm, but she was like many Russians I'd met [after the Revolution]. She was haunted by not having enough money. Dalí was her gold-mine and she was afraid of losing it. In that sense, she was savagely Russian.' If Gala thought of Dalí as her gold-mine, she had to labour hard to make it pay. Even before meeting Dalí, the prince had enthused about his art to his aristocratic friends, the Vicomte de Noailles and his wife, Marie-Laure. The Noailleses were to become Dalí's most loyal benefactors, saving him from extreme poverty.

In early January 1930 Dalí and Gala left Paris. They spent two months alone together in a hotel at Carry-le-Rouet, in southern France, with the shutters closed, a stack of wood for the fireplace, a few books, paints, canvas and an easel. They would open the door a crack for a chambermaid to bring the meals. 'Gala understood that we had to flee the world so as to temper ourselves as a couple in the crucible of life alone together,' wrote Dalí. It was in that room that Dalí's maniacal gaze devoured Gala for the first time, that he atomised her and initiated the process of re-creating her, in his vision, on his canvas. The way Dalí described it, their intense confinement in bed by a burning hearth seemed to be the source of his hundreds of Gala portraits. He also, in his own words, became 'a sex freak'. In *The Unspeakable Confessions of Salvador Dalí* he writes:

> I fixed in my memory the value of every grain of her skin so as to apprehend the shadings of their consistency and colour; so as to find the right attentive caress. . . . I spent hours looking at her breasts, their curve, the design of the nipples, the shadings of pink to their tips, the detail of the bluish

veinlets running beneath their gossamer transparency; her back ravished me with the delicacy of the joints, the strength of the rump muscles, beauty and beast conjoined. Her neck had pure grace in its slimness; her hair, her intimate hair, her odours intoxicated me.

Gala did not entirely shut herself off from the world. She still saw fit to write to Eluard, slipping in her address at Carry-le-Rouet on the Riviera. His response to her conveys his growing desperation and fear of losing her permanently. 'Very slowly I'm getting bored with you (a grand melancholy, a great resigned emptiness).' His next letter shows no such resignation: 'I want you so much. I'm going mad. I die at the very idea of returning to you, of seeing you, of kissing you. I want it so that your hand, your mouth, your sex never leaves my sex.' Eluard expected that Gala would reply immediately, and when she did not he became almost suicidal over her loss. Two weeks later he wrote: 'Gala, if the thought comes to me that all could be finished between us, I truly feel like someone condemned to death, and what a death.' The sentence is heavily underscored for emphasis, even though Eluard was involved in simultaneous affairs with Nusch and a pretty German, Madame Apfel.

Dalí received at least one letter that jarred them both out of their Riviera hibernation. It was from the Vicomte de Noailles, warning Dalí that Camille Goëmans had run out of money and was shutting down his gallery. Fortunately, the vicomte was so impressed by Dalí's art that he offered to buy his next canvas. Gala swung into action. She volunteered to extract what she could of the funds that Goëmans owed Dalí. Hopeless in financial matters, Dalí gratefully agreed and Gala went off to Paris.

Carry-le-Rouet was not far from Hyères, where Charles and Marie-Laure de Noailles had their winter villa. Together Dalí and Gala had elaborated a plan: while Gala was in Paris trying to recover the money owed by Goëmans, Dalí would ask the Vicomte de Noailles for enough money to buy a small house in Cadaqués where he could paint the only landscape that had ever moved him. Alone, wearing a dapper white suit that Gala had doubtless chosen for him, Dalí arrived at Hyères, an austere modernistic villa built by one of Le Corbusier's disciples high on a terraced hill covered with almond trees. Charles and Marie-Laure de Noailles were quite taken by Dalí's pathetic timidity –

they called him 'le petit Dalí' – and wrote him a cheque for 29,000 francs. It was nothing for them; they had put up the colossal sum of over one million francs for Buñuel to make L'Age d'or. None the less, it was more money than Dalí had ever dreamed of holding at one time. He and Gala met back at the hotel and she too had succeeded in securing a small payment from the bankrupt Goëmans. Before going back to Paris, they accepted an invitation from the de Noailles to spend a few days with them at Hyères.

Charles and Marie-Laure were a strange couple. Marie-Laure was a descendant of the Marquis de Sade, and one of her most prized possessions was her ancestor's original manuscript of 120 Days of Sodom, rolled inside a huge leather phallus. Charles never let slip his aristocratic façade, though he too was very much taken by the antics of their eccentric guests. Visitors to Hyères were free to disport themselves as they liked under one condition: that they indulge in the de Noailles' passion for fitness. There are snapshots of André Gide gamely hanging from his heels inside a giant hoop, Jean Cocteau heaving a fat leather medicine ball at the resident gymnastics coach, the sculptor Lipschitz with Victor Hugo's grandson playing miniature golf on a course set among the almond trees. Gala and Dalí were not great sports; physically Dalí was a coward.

Henri Sauguet, a French composer, occupied one of the de Noailles' dozen guest rooms at the same time Gala and Dalí were there, but they had little time for him. Music was considered a minor art by the surrealists. 'Dalí said that music didn't convey anything as real as eggs on a plate,' Sauguet reported. 'I replied that music could make you *feel* the eggs were there.' The sole form of exercise taken by Dalí and Gala, recalls Sauguet, seems to have been groping each other on the salon couch. Their conduct was considered tasteless. 'The de Noailles were liberal, but this was exhibitionism,' said the composer. 'Their hands and lips were never apart. They were playing *grand amour*.'

Gala quickly caught on that Marie-Laure was as flighty as she was extravagant with gestures and promises. She craved attention from her assembled court of artists and writers. 'Charles was noble and cold but if you wanted money he was the one to go to,' Sauguet observed. 'Marie-Laure made promises but never kept them. She was in perpetual motion.'

Gala impressed the vicomte with her savoir-faire. De Noailles later remarked of Gala to Sauguet that 'Dalí wouldn't be where he was without Gala.' There was a startling difference between the de Noailles' first impression of Dalí as a painfully shy young man and the second, that of an outrageous exhibitionist. Gala gave Dalí the strength to assert his latent showmanship. Sauguet, who had first met Gala with Eluard, was astonished at the change in her. 'She had become Dalínian. It was though she let her personality become lost inside Dalí's.'

8

Hungrier Than An Andalucian Dog

After Hyères, Gala stayed in Paris long enough to tell Eluard she was leaving him. Then, clutching the Vicomte de Noailles' cheque, Gala and Dalí decided to head south. Dalí's desire to buy a fisherman's shack at Port Lligat, a black and still lagoon over the hill from Cadaqués, had grown into an obsession. He wanted to do it quickly before he frittered away the money or, more likely, lost the cheque. Once in Cadaqués, though, Dalí received a shock. Dalí's father had imposed his will with a vengeance; he wanted his son's suffering to be complete.

Gala and Dalí were accorded a grim reception. The owner of Cadaqués's only hotel, the Miramar, refused them a room. To do otherwise would have invited scandal. Salvador, after all, was a local boy and local boys did not check into hotels with married women. Dalí was convinced that the Miramar's owner was acting on instructions from his angry father. Salvador was not without charm, however, and one of his father's old servants took pity and secretly sheltered the couple in town. The hostility they encountered everywhere hastened their desire to move to Port Lligat. 'The only people with whom I was interested in keeping on good terms were the dozen fishermen of Port Lligat,' wrote Dalí.

Life in a solitary stone hut, as Dalí envisaged it, was so primitive that Gala must have been genuinely in love to have accompanied him. The hardships were daunting: the winter sea dampness churned through Gala's weak lungs; she did not speak the chattering Catalan language; and she was being asked to trade a luxurious flat with a view of all Paris for the confines of a one-room shack with no electric light, no heat and no water. In addition, Dalí worked incessantly. Either Gala must learn to share Dalí's monastic devotion to art, his art, or she would go crazy.

It was a hard walk from Cadaqués to Port Lligat, one that Dalí and Gala always made in daytime. The path threaded by a cemetery, and Dalí was afraid of graveyard ghosts. The shack they had bought with the vicomte's money was pathetically small. It was little more than a windbreak from the fierce Tramontana, a place where the fishermen could huddle together and bait their hooks while they drank wine. In its present state, the hut was so filthy and bare that the fishermen, drunk though they may have been, preferred climbing the hill back to their homes in Cadaqués to sleeping there. The location, however, was spectacular. Lines of olive trees, shimmering silver, rose on steps up the black hills. The waves and the sea winds were fended off by a peninsula of sheared meteoric-looking rock, giving the little lagoon a kind of charged tranquillity, like the eye of a hurricane. It was not pretty, but intense.

Gala threw herself into the work with Dalí of making the place habitable. A carpenter was hired to add a kitchen galley and tiny bathroom to their shack. The work, however, would take several weeks to finish, and in the meantime the winter cold and the equally icy treatment given them by the townspeople were taking their toll. Gala awoke one morning to find herself coughing painfully at every breath. She had fallen ill with pleurisy.

Fortunately, Gala and Dalí were in Barcelona at the time the infection struck, and she was able to receive good medical care. Dalí was hardly responsive to her every need. In fact, he panicked. The luminous pallor of her fever filled him with anxiety and yet, at the same time, it excited a dangerous urge to extinguish her, to smother her with kisses and crush her like a small flower in his hands. 'Her illness had given her such a fragile look that when one saw her in her tea-rose nightgown she looked like one of those fairies drawn by Raphael Kishner that seemed on the point of dying from the mere effort of smelling one of the decorative gardenias twice as large and as heavy as their heads,' wrote Dalí.

What Gala needed was to keep warm and stay in bed. Instead, Dalí forced her out into the night air, to a park, where he dragged her up a long flight of stairs so that she could see a fairground's coloured lights and fireworks. Her reaction was extraordinary. It might have been the delirium of her pleurisy, or Gala's desire for high-voltage experiences, undimmed by illness, but as she watched the spectacle she exclaimed: 'You know how to do everything for me! You make me weep all the time!'

If Dalí knew what was good for Gala's psyche, his lack of nursing skills was also enough to make her weep. The doctors had prescribed warmth, so Dalí took their advice to a dangerous extreme. He decided the perfect cure would be a trip to Málaga, many miles south in Andalucía. With Gala's history of lung infections, it would have been sensible for her to spend several months convalescing. Eluard, who himself had had one lung removed, was desperately worried for her. Despite their break-up, she had written to him of her illness. His reply was frantic. 'I cried with worry. My hair has gone white. . . . Be very careful!' Instead, just a few days after Gala first fell ill with pleurisy, Dalí subjected her to a long and gruelling train ride across Spain. They travelled second-class. 'She remained for hours with her cheek glued against my chest, and I was astonished that her small head, which seemed to be composed wholly of expression, should be so heavy. It was as if the whole little cranium were filled with lead.'

Despite her frail health, Gala never complained, never capitalised on it to make Dalí do her bidding. Her struggle with poor health was intensely private. She did not want to recognise this weakness in herself, and she certainly would have disdained the pity of others.

The train arrived in Málaga at siesta time, and then she and Dalí travelled by tram down the coast. The driver was drunk on anise and sang as the tram clattered across a bridge over marshes until they reached their destination: Torremolinos. In those days it was not a tourist resort. It had no hotels, only small fishermen's cottages much like the one that was to be Gala's and Dalí's home in Port Lligat. They rented a cottage on a sea cliff surrounded by red carnations, and the scenery as much as the warm temperatures aided Gala's recovery.

Gala and Dalí fitted in with the uninhibitedness of the fishermen and the colony of gypsies who lived half-naked in sea caves. With her small breasts and short-cropped hair, Gala was able to sunbathe topless on the Torremolinos beach – a good forty years before other tourists would dare – or so Dalí claimed. She swam, and helped Dalí prepare the final draft of his book,

Visible Woman. The cottage had room only for Dalí's easel and a narrow bed with a lumpy mattress.

Meanwhile Gala was feeling the tug of Eluard's affections. A torrent of letters began arriving from him, many of them erotic. Eluard explained how he had been consoling himself by browsing through the many nude photographs he had taken of Gala: 'You have the most beautiful eyes in the world, I love you, you take my sex in your hand, your legs are spread, your body sinks softly, you stroke me furiously, I crush your breasts, your hair, and suddenly your hand is full of sperm and you are strong and sure of my power over you, of your power over me, over Everything. You are still the troubled infant of Clavadel.' It was in the health spa of Clavadel that they first met, and it is touching that Eluard, after all the hurt they caused each other, still treasured that early memory of Gala. One wonders whether she hid Eluard's ardent letters from Dalí or read them aloud to him.

Eluard's ejaculations of love must have disturbed Gala. She was still susceptible to him and possibly still desired him. After all, Dalí made no secret that masturbating was more epiphanous than sex with Gala. The troubled girl of Clavadel had, after all, deserted Russia and her family for Eluard. She had had a child by him, and had helped his poetic powers grow. But Gala had a capacity, both terrible and heroic, for amputating her old emotional ties when they tangled with new ones. She had done this with her family to join Eluard; she was now preparing to cut herself off from Eluard and her daughter for Dalí.

The opportunity had come. Eluard wrote: 'If you can only love me weakly, you must tell me.' If Eluard had meant it as a routine reassurance, Gala did not. Her blunt reply – by telegram – stunned Eluard 'stupid'. His pain was all the more acute because his dalliance with the German girl, Madame Apfel, or 'Pomme' as he called her, had ended. The apartment on the rue Becquerel that he had found and decorated for Gala, with its portraits of her, her dresses, her scent bottles in the bathroom, became unbearable for Eluard. It was a mockery of all his plans of domestic reunion. If he could have afforded it, he would have moved into a hotel. It was the end, he wrote, to 'all that I dreamt about: where to take you, your dresses, your pleasure, your sleep, your dreams, all that I did clumsily, all that I wanted to repair [between us]. . . . I know well that I cannot keep you, that the abomination of married life has finished us, but it seems to me that I have not had you for years.'

Blunt though Gala was, she also had practical reasons for not severing completely with her husband. Eluard had money; she and Dalí did not. Moreover, he was a powerful ally in the art world. Already, Eluard had intervened on Dalí's behalf with Breton. To illustrate a book by Breton, Dalí had submitted a drawing of a man indulging in his own favourite pastime – masturbation. The prudish Breton was appalled but too embarrassed to tell Dalí so directly; Eluard took on the diplomatic task himself. Dalí and Gala needed somewhere to live when they returned to Paris, and there was always his apartment on the rue Becquerel. After all, Eluard said he found it intolerable to live there.

Gala continued to observe several marital niceties important to Eluard. In Málaga she bought kitsch postcards for her husband's collection. Although Gala never bothered about what others thought of her behaviour, she humoured Eluard, who cared a great deal, and agreed to write to her mother-in-law with an excuse that Eluard had concocted to explain her long absence. Gala was to tell her that the trip to Málaga had been for health reasons, and that she was staying there as the guest of Eluard's friends. It was basically a variation on the lie that Eluard had used to cover his Asian escapade and was probably transparent to Eluard's mother.

After telling Eluard that their marriage was finished, Gala seems suddenly to have recanted. Either she had misgivings about Dalí – over their unsatisfactory sex life, perhaps – or there was a more callous reason: Eluard, with his influence and inheritance, was of use to them. She dashed off a letter to Eluard vowing that she 'desired violently to see him'. After her previous rejection of him, Eluard was confused and somewhat suspicious of her motives. He also made it clear that Gala and Dalí could not squat at the rue Becquerel. The crash on Wall Street had resounded mightily in Paris. Eluard had lost money on the Paris Bourse, and the reverses of his rich clients meant they could not afford to buy the art and primitive statuary that Eluard retailed. Moreover, their daughter Cécile was diagnosed as suffering from a severe spinal disorder; the little cash that Eluard had remaining went on Cécile's hospital bills. Eluard explained to Gala that he had no choice but to get rid of the apartment.

It wasn't long before the money which Gala had borrowed

from Eluard to live on in Málaga ran out. The only food that remained was stale bread and a few drops of olive oil smelling of anchovies. Their friend and benefactor, someone Dalí had known from his Madrid student days, had departed suddenly from Málaga, and Dalí refused Gala's entreaties to have the Vicomte de Noailles' cheque sent down from the safe in the Barcelona hotel where they had left it. Their poverty was entirely of Dalí's doing, and in a pique he contemplated abandoning Gala to live with the gypsies. Instead, he stalked out to the middle of the carnation field and masturbated. Feeling silly about his behaviour afterwards, Dalí punished himself in a childish frenzy. He pummelled his face so hard with his fists that he broke a tooth.

Exultantly, he ran back to Gala, who had all Dalí's suits and trousers spread about the cottage, searching for stray coins.

'Guess!'

'A glow-worm,' she said, knowing that I was fond of gathering them.

'No! My tooth – I broke my little tooth; we must by all means go and put it in Cadaqués, hang it by a thread in the centre of our house in Port Lligat.'

Gala had come to accept Dalí's logic of omens and baby teeth. She began packing their suitcases, but the dilemma remained: just because Dalí felt it was an auspicious time to return to Cadaqués, it didn't mean that money would materialise to make this possible. Eventually, a communist friend lent them 50 pesetas which kept them alive until their money was wired from Barcelona. Dalí had relented and agreed to cash the vicomte's cheque.

As it happened, Gala and Dalí spent only two hours in Cadaqués. They were demoralised at how little work had been done on their home and decided to return to Paris. There was a practical reason for going: Dalí could try to secure new contracts.

Paris, in the meantime, had forgotten Dalí. The buyers were not forthcoming. His success of the previous autumn had guttered out with surprising swiftness. It was not that Eluard had poisoned the surrealists and art critics against his wife's lover. To his credit, he never let his anguish cross his genuine admiration for Dalí's art. This admiration, though, was no longer universally shared. Suddenly Dalí's classical treatment of sexual anxieties had fallen from vogue. Picasso's primitivism was in. The native art of Africa was being rediscovered. Nobody wanted Dalí's baroque intellectuality, his subversion of Old Masters, and it crushed him.

To make matters worse, some of Dalí's paintings were destroyed. Buñuel had gone ahead and filmed L'Age d'or without Dalí, who thought Buñuel's rabid anti-clericalism could have been less dogmatic. L'Age d'or was screened at Studio 28, near the surrealists' café in the Place Blanche, and caused a huge uproar. The Vicomte de Noailles, who had financed the film, was blackballed from the snobbish Jockey Club and threatened by the Pope with excommunication. During one showing, a gang of reactionary youths, the Camelots du Roi, stormed the theatre, bashing the audience with clubs and slashing paintings by Yves Tanguy and Dalí exhibited in the foyer.

This black period hardened Gala. She suffered Dalí's rejection as deeply as he did. Dalí had a few commissions, but at the time he laboured with a miniaturist's perfection on each canvas. Each painting had to be a work of genius; he had to prove his detractors wrong. In the meantime, however, Dalí desperately needed another source of income. With typical zaniness, he decided to become an inventor, a twentieth-century Leonardo da Vinci. They could no longer squat at Eluard's. Dalí and Gala rented a studio near a railway yard. Their kitchen table was littered with designs of plastic mannequins filled with swimming goldfish, shoes with springs, dresses with breasts protruding from the back, false fingernails with mirrors. As soon as each design was finished, Gala would grab the drawing and trudge down to the centre of Paris from their flat in a Montparnasse cul-de-sac. She tried buttonholing haute-couture designers – friends who soon became former friends – department-store executives, anyone who might be remotely interested in Dalí's uncomfortable and outlandish creations. No one was. After countless visits, Gala was seldom allowed past the receptionists. She grew frustrated and vengeful. 'I hate the Jews,' Gala later told one American collector, 'because they would always try to feel me up before they'd buy a painting. Just because I was the artist's woman they thought I'd do anything to sell his work. I didn't think of it.'

Gala later struck back. This same American collector, Reynolds Morse, remembers visiting Gala's suite during the 1960s at the

St Regis in New York City. 'My wife, Eleanor, and I had brought Gala a small bouquet of flowers. But her room was already filled with huge, ornate displays from the best florists in New York. There was an expensive silver fish that came with one arrangement. I asked Gala who had sent all the flowers and she replied: "They're from the Jewish dealers. They know it's the only way I'll think of giving them a contract with Dali." '

Behind her back, the dealers called her Gala la Gale, a French wordplay, since *gale* has two meanings – a spiteful person and scabies, an irritating skin disease.

Many artists had their studios nearby, but Gala and Dalí lived like hermits. This was partly because they were self-conscious about their poverty, but also because Dalí simply never stopped working. He was determined to paint so magnificently that his genius would finally be impossible to ignore; either that or, wrote Dalí, 'our fate would be literally to die of hunger'.

Gala and Dalí did manage to outlast the 1930–31 Paris winter. They had received word from Cadaqués that the carpenter had finished work on their small house. It was, at last, habitable. They packed up the essentials only: an easel, painting supplies, the few pieces of modernist furniture they had bought second-hand or had given to them by Eluard, gas heaters – the stone hut had no electricity – a glass-encased butterfly and insect collection and a spine-snapping weight of textbooks. Dalí was enthralled by science.

He had not succeeded in winning over the Paris art world, but he had resown the seeds of interest in his extraordinary talent. The moment had come for a strategic retreat, one that would test Gala's devotion to Dalí even further. The Dalí family feud with their son had poisoned the townspeople of Cadaqués against her. She was the foreign woman, the corrupter, the whore. Worse, though, in many ways was the prospect of being closed up with Dalí in quarters no larger than a prison cell.

It was as if Dalí were a child in the perpetual state of awakening from a nightmare, one in which he was being menaced by giant grasshoppers, the distorted spectres of sexual paranoia, and death wearing a thousand faces. In this anxiety-ridden universe, Gala was to become Dalí's only guide and protector.

9

Instructing The Fishermen

Gala's health was frail. A year after falling ill with pleurisy, her recovery was still not complete; her breathing was still laboured and the doctors in Barcelona, where Dalí had rushed her from Cadaqués, could not discover why. The medical fees had sapped their meagre resources and they decided to return to Paris in early 1931 and try to sell Dalí's new canvases. Borrowing money from Eluard, Gala consulted Parisian specialists and finally, after a battery of X-rays and tests, a diagnosis was reached. The doctors had found a fibrous tumour growing inside her lung. The tumour had to be removed.

That winter in Paris, while Gala was undergoing surgery, Dalí paced the streets, frantic. He had built his sanity around Gala, conquered his many fears with her firm clarity, her conviction that, together, their destiny would be sublime. He even believed that Gala was his talisman against death. Yet, if she were to die under the surgeon's knife, all of that carefully constructed cathedral of security would fall. He relied on her for everything: meals, buying train tickets, selling his paintings and even choosing his clothes. Dalí could not bring himself to visit her in hospital; her mortality – and his own – terrified him too much.

Gala not only survived the operation, but grew far healthier than before. The tumour had been the root cause of all the lung problems that had plagued her since adolescence. She was thirty-six, Dalí ten years younger.

However, she was not so fortunate with another operation which also took place in the first months of 1931. Doctors had located a second tumour, this time in her uterus. Its removal was an especially barbarous procedure, and when Gala described the operation to a friend nearly forty years later the experience was still so painful in her mind that she cried. The doctors, she said, had 'emptied' her.

Ernesto Gimenez Caballero, a Madrid friend of Dalí's who visited them in Paris while Gala was still recovering, remembers her unkindly as 'that woman without sex, violent and sterile'. Even if she had wanted to, Gala could no longer bear any more children. For many months, she was also too scarred to make love. Dalí in 1930 painted a canvas which was oddly prescient of Gala's surgery. Entitled *Bleeding Roses*, it shows a blonde whose lean body is obviously Gala's, with a womb of roses that are bleeding on to her sex. The blood falls like teardrops.

Rafael Santos Torroella, an art critic and longstanding friend of Dalí and Gala, speculates that this sterilisation may have been at the root of her nymphomania: 'She was constantly needing to prove her feminine identity.' However, her affairs with Ernst, de Chirico and numerous other men suggest that her libidinousness was in full flower long before the operation.

There is no mention of this trauma in her letters to Eluard, but she spoke openly of it to her male acquaintances. Henri Pastoureau, a university student who gravitated into the surrealist circle, regularly attended 'sexual investigation' sessions in 1933 with Gala and Dalí. Other women were barred by Gala from these Wednesday evening explorations into the participants' sexual behaviour and fantasies. 'She wouldn't hesitate to describe, in the crudest details, her wildest debaucheries,' said Pastoureau. 'But she always added that surgery had stopped her from continuing with this.'

Gala usually held the floor in these 'sexual investigations', while, according to Pastoureau, 'Dalí was almost always quiet unless he had some new and delirious fantasy, always of a scatological kind.' In all likelihood, Gala and Dalí both benefited from these sessions. For Dalí it was a socially acceptable way of releasing his childish, anal obsessions. Gala, at the same time, was able to compensate for whatever inadequacies may have been caused by the French doctors' surgery by being the sexual ringmaster – if only verbally – with the young men in attendance. Pastoureau claims that Gala regaled them with tales of her sexual exploits in 'meticulous detail', and that her lovers were always men: 'She was neither a lesbian nor bisexual.'

While the other participants in this odd game were repelled by Dalí's fixation with excrement, Gala was not. She encouraged

Dalí's scatological talk until he became positively lyrical. This could be another example of how Gala coaxed him into becoming less shy about his sexual inadequacies, which in turn stimulated his creativity. Her mission with Dalí, as she interpreted it, was to provide the ideal conditions for his art to flourish; she learned how to prepare his canvases, purchase and mix his paints, feed him, care for him and treat his sexual aberrations with tolerance. Dalí's latrinalian fetishes still appeared in his canvases but he was no longer their captive.

Later, Dalí's success allowed him the opportunity to flesh out these titillating verbal encounters. There were plenty of live models willing to act out his fantasies for money and to seize the chance of joining his strange court of admirers. Through the years, though, Gala became sickened by the babyish exhibitionism of Dalí's 'erotic masses', as he called them, and she would always absent herself.

If Gala's love-making had been impaired by surgery, it was not permanent. Pastoureau recalled one evening: 'I saw her leave Dalí in the middle of an austere discussion with Breton. She took her pleasure with Eluard on a divan, in the shadows under the arcade. One can think that Gala was not only acting out her carnal desire for Eluard, whom she had obviously not forgotten, but also because she was trying to provoke Breton, whom she detested. She was trying to provoke all of us.'

That summer, Dalí brought Gala back to Cadaqués to convalesce. This was to set a pattern that, apart from during two wars, they would adhere to always: that is, they spent the spring and summer months in Port Lligat, over the hill from Cadaqués, and the remainder of the year travelling, socialising and burnishing Dalí's public image.

For the villagers of Cadaqués, the return of Dalí and Gala must have seemed like a travelling carnival. Donkeys had been hired to haul their odd belongings over the hill to Port Lligat. There were strange insects in glass cases, lamps like steel masks, books of marvellous towers and palaces and, of course, his paintings. One imagines children running alongside the donkeys exclaiming over the paintings jutting from the panniers as they caught sight of lions' heads, a naked woman with a knife, and familiar shapes that could have been the stones of Cape Creus turned to flesh.

Port Lligat seemed a good choice. The summer was warm and fragrant with yellow and purple wild flowers. The coastal mountains no longer seemed a citadel of stone, forbidding and barren, but had been splashed by colour. It was just as well that the weather was clement, for once Gala and Dalí had spread the contents of their ten suitcases about their home the only standing room was in front of the easel. It was a revolving wooden easel, and in that small cabin Dalí stood before it like a fisherman at the helm, navigating uncharted seas. Gala occupied herself with less glamorous chores. She fetched water from a spring beside the blooming oleander bushes of the creek, battled with invasions of flies and ants, and imposed an order on the chaos of sketches, pages ripped from scientific magazines, paints and brushes with which Dalí surrounded himself. She had to drop everything and come to Dalí's help whenever a grasshopper hopped into the room. Grasshoppers terrified Dalí.

Gala was a kind of Sancho Panza to Dalí's mad Quixote; she was entranced by his wild visions but retained enough common sense to distinguish windmills from giants, monsters from grasshoppers. It is telling that Dalí's first portrait of Gala, executed on a white doily, has her peering out of a seashell, as secretive as the ocean sounds captured inside its spirals. Outside Gala's shell are a grasshopper and a squirrel (one of her pet names). Several more years would pass before Dalí dared to undertake a major portrait of her.

They were miserably poor. They bought fish and sea urchins off the boats and were helped around the kitchen by an amiable madwoman, Lydia, whom Dalí found amusing. It was a good half-hour's walk over the hill to Cadaqués for other goods, and each trip was touched with panic. They did not want to run into Dalí's father or sister. Dalí's father viewed his son's move to Port Lligat with anger; it seemed an act of rebellion, which was the last thing on Dalí's mind – all that Dalí wanted was a place of quiet inspiration. The break with his family had hurt him to the quick, and he did not want to infuriate his father any more. On walks up on the ridge overlooking Cadaqués, Gala and Dalí looked down on his father's white house, set against the serpentine hills, with longing and unease. The house, he wrote, 'seemed like a piece of sugar – sugar soaked in gall.' Avoiding his father and sister was easy enough, though, since the Dalí family summered on the far side of Cadaqués. Ana Maria, the

77

sister, was a church-goer, and Gala and Dalí learned to time their trek over the hill so they would arrive during mass.

Snapshots of the period show Gala as boyish and sensibly dressed. She wore men's shoes, and shorts or trousers. She stopped curling her hair and wore it in a pageboy style. If she went topless, as she had in Torremolinos, it was probably done with caution. The gossips would have quickly spread word of such infamy back to the eager ears of his father and Ana Maria. The family was still convinced that Gala was a dissolute Russian who had roped Dalí into her ring of drug smugglers. Catalina Romans, who worked as a maid in the artist's home, said: 'There were two people whose names we were forbidden to mention: Dalí's sister, Ana Maria and Gala's daughter, Cécile.'

One indication of the intensity of the wrath Dalí's father felt towards his son and Gala surfaces in a letter he wrote to Dalí's closest school friend, Federico García Lorca, the poet. Dalí's father describes his son as 'perfectly shameless . . . his indignity has reached the extreme of accepting money and food given to him by a married woman who, with the consent and approval of her husband, has him well baited so that at the opportune moment they can give him the push. You can imagine the pain that all this rubbish has caused.'

Occasionally, to celebrate the completion of a painting or an article for Breton's provocative magazine, *Surréalisme au service de la révolution*, Dalí and Gala would sail with the fishermen over to the coves of Cape Creus for a picnic of grilled fish or lamb chops with freshly picked rosemary. As they rowed slowly over the still water, Dalí would enthusiastically point out to Gala how the shape of the rocks slowly metamorphosed: an angel became a camel or a lion; an eagle domesticated itself into a farmhouse rooster. It was, said Dalí, 'like living in a constant mirage . . . and yet, when we land, the granite beneath our feet is hard, compact, clear, implacable.'

Frequently Dalí and Gala would head south down the coast to the large *masia* – or country mansion – of another Catalan artist, José-Maria Sert, and his wife, Roussy, a Russian noblewoman and sculptor. Sert, who painted on commission from kings and princes around Europe, was fabulously wealthy, and he often took Dalí and Gala on cruises around the coast in a yacht shaped like a Venetian shoe. Bettina Bergery, a bright and beautiful American model who was one of Gala's few women friends, sailed with them once. She recalled: 'Gala could read the mind of Dalí and of most people. She did everything for him – I'm sure she even brushed his teeth. There was no doubt she was in love with Dalí, but as a sister with a brother. When things went wrong, she never scolded Dalí. She didn't have to. She just looked sad or contemptuous. That was enough.'

Madame Bergery said that Gala shared Dalí's sense of the absurd. 'René Clair's bathing costume was drying on a clothes line. Gala pinned a flopping fish next to it. Another time, we docked in a small village. I climbed on a donkey in my shorts and began to ride through the streets. Then Dalí and Gala came running alongside and wouldn't stop licking my legs,' she recounted. 'Gala allowed herself to be dressed by Dalí and she always looked extraordinary. On anyone else the outfit would've looked absurd. Maybe it was because of her eyes. With women she had the most questioning, challenging eyes. With men, the same eyes became gentle.'

At Port Lligat there were times when Gala would sail out alone with a fisherman for the sole purpose of having sex. Bettina Bergery remarked: 'There was a slight problem. Dalí was too busy saving his libido for painting, and Gala liked to make love. She had a great deal of experience at it, too, and she ended up teaching love's acrobatics to the young fishermen.' These amorous cruises were the perfect solution. They were private; she and her novice lover could drop anchor in any one of a dozen secluded coves. There were smooth, warm sandstone hollows to lie in, or a place for a blanket in the shade of a poisonous oleander. Sometimes Gala would bring back a lobster that had scuttled into her submerged trap while she was making love. In this way, Dalí was spared the trauma of witnessing her infidelity and Gala could relieve herself of the unhappiness involved in sharing Dalí's bed. It was a cosy arrangement that, with subtle variations, would last throughout their fifty-three years together.

Gala's young fishermen have grown old, but they still dock their small blue and white boats on the stone quay beside Dalí's home. The entrails of gutted fish and octopus float beside their boats. 'Gala?' one fisherman named Santos told me. 'Yes, I've known her since I was a boy. I can't really say much. You see, Señor Dalí has been good to us.' It seems that Gala also prized her young fishermen for their discretion. In the village of Cadaqués, though, the story is told that Gala never forgave anyone who rejected her advances, and as she grew older the list of those who spurned her grew longer. There were young men in Cadaqués who fled when she approached, even though she rewarded her favourites with money, signed doodles by Dalí or important contracts for work.

Acquaintances say that Dalí knew of Gala's dalliances and took a vicarious delight in them. In this respect, Dalí and Eluard were remarkably similar; they were both voyeurs, and Gala was only too willing to oblige them. Eluard's clinging to Gala had its perverse side. The relationship with Dalí was tolerated as long as Gala shared in the details, made Eluard feel as though he were sitting on a couch in the same room watching it all. In one remarkable letter, which Eluard wrote from his mother's house, he demanded that she send nude photos of herself. 'The night before last, there was a great stripe of moonlight in the room and I really saw you all naked with your legs spread and you were being taken by two men, in the mouth and in your sex. And you were brown and beautiful. And now, over this memory, I dream that you are for me the incarnation of love, the sharpest incarnation of desire and erotic pleasure. You are all my imagination.' Further on he complained: 'Why haven't you taken those nude photos of yourself? And I would like to have some of where you make love. And I will make love with you in front of Nusch, who will only be able to stroke herself – and all that you want.'

This erotic outburst came after several letters in which Eluard was perceptibly cold to her; these letters are dutiful, filled with his buying and mainly selling of art. Even his sign-offs of love are crisp and formal. It seems likely that Gala may have written in the meantime, encouraging Eluard or even expressing her dissatisfaction with Dalí as a lover.

His letter is all the more surprising in its ardour because earlier Eluard had asked Gala for a divorce. He had wanted to marry Nusch, whom he relegates to a solitary spectator in his love-making fantasies. If Eluard wrote to Gala about his desire to marry the waif-like Nusch, Gala chose not to keep the letter. Rarely in this correspondence does Eluard ever mention his new wife. Nusch seems to be pliant enough to take Eluard's pining for Gala without jealousy, so the more likely explanation is that Eluard did not mention his new bride in the letters because Gala was opposed to his remarriage. Gala's instinctive reaction to other women was dislike, especially those who represented a

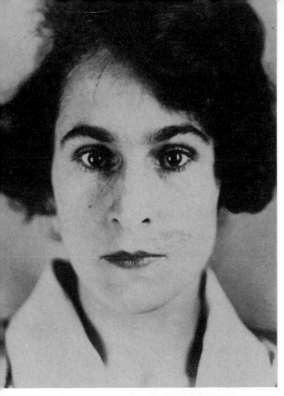

1927. Gala, by Man Ray. Her eyes were her most magnetic feature. Her gaze, wrote Eluard, could 'pierce walls'. (The Man Ray Archive)

Gala and Eluard, both 17, met as patients at the Clavadel sanatorium in the Swiss Alps. They remained in love even after Gala returned to her family in Russia and Eluard to his in Paris. (Rene-Jacques)

Eluard, Dalì in a diver's suit and Gala, at the First International Surrealist Exhibition, London in 1936. (© Lee Miller Archives)

Dalì, with Gala and Herbert Read, at the Exhibition. Dalì's pechant for show-business made him rich but earned him the other surrealists' envy and abuse. (© Lee Miller Archives)

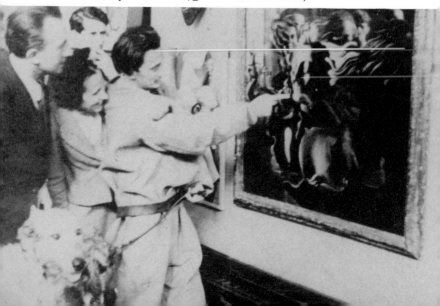

In the 1940s Surrealism went high-society. Fancy dress balls were organised by the wealthy, with Dalì and Gala as star guests. Here they are at a Bad Dreams Party in Del Monte, California. (Wide World Photos)

During a photo session with Cecil Beaton during the 1940s. (Sotheby's)

Together at the
Brown Derby,
Hollywood, in the
1940s. Even the film
industry was hit by
surrealist mania.
Dalì traded
surrealist jokes with
the Marx brothers,
designed sets for
Hitchcock and
painted film moguls,
for huge fees.
(UPI/Bettmann
Newsphotos)

During the war Gala
and Dalì fled Europe
and settled in
Monterey,
California, whose
wild coast reminded
Dalì of his native
Catalonia.
(UPI/Bettman
Newsphotos)

On board the USS *America* just after the war on 24 December. (Wide World Photos)

Lunch for Gala and Dalì was often sea urchins fetched from the deep waters off Cape Creus and always eaten raw. (Oriol Maspons, Barcelona)

This round room with its Turkish divans was Gala's favourite seduction scene. Dalì would disappear on cue. (Hulton Picture Library)

As this photo was being snapped, Dalì saw Gala sailing out to sea with a lover. 'I'm the king of the cuckolds,' he said. (Oriol Maspons, Barcelona)

Dalì's fears excluded all sexual activity but masturbation. He was a voyeur repelled by physical contact with women. (Hulton Picture Library)

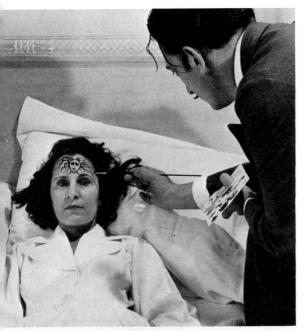

Dalì painted his muse hundreds of times, on canvas and on her flesh. He was not always flattering; here he applies a Medusa to Gala's forehead. (Robert Hunt Library)

When Gala was in her late
seventies, she fell so madly in
love with Jeff Fenholt – who
played Jesus Christ Superstar
in the Broadway version –
that she was prepared to
abandon Dalì. (Lincoln
Center Picture Library)

When Gala dies, Dalì fell
apart. Her name reminded
him of his own impending
death. He retreated to Gala's
private castle, closed the
curtains and turned away
food and drink.
(UPI/Bettmann Newsphotos)

threat – as Nusch did. Nusch was pretty, young and animated, and a grateful slave to Eluard's caprices. After all, she had been found on the street by Eluard, cold and starving, and taken in like a stray puppy. Eluard could not have chosen a more different replacement for Gala.

However, Gala had other reasons: she simply did not want to lose her hold on Eluard. She was proud to be desired by him. When Gala was in her fifties, she met Eluard after a long absence and said: 'I have a present for you. Here.' With that, she pulled open her blouse so that Eluard could have the pleasure of caressing her breast. Eluard did not refuse the invitation.

There was one person who actively opposed Gala's formal separation from Eluard – their daughter, Cécile. Although she was brought up by Eluard's wealthy mother, Cécile clung to Gala - or tried to. One can imagine the sense of abandonment the girl must have felt over her mother's long trips and even longer silences. Cécile worshipped her father, who at weekends pampered her with excursions to films, gave her poetry books and was kind and solicitous towards her. She also saw that he was wounded by Gala's departure.

Cécile was a young teenager when Eluard and Gala finally decided to break up, old enough to sense the problems that had arisen between her parents through veiled remarks by her grandmother, knowledge of her father's flirtatious women companions and her mother's mysterious absences. These were the sort of disquieting things to brood about alone in a room in her grandmother's villa when she watched her father's car disappear down the lane.

At the height of the Eluard family drama, Gala's sister, Lidia, arrived from Russia. Lidia remembers that Cécile appealed for Gala to stay with them. Crying, the girl told her mother that Eluard genuinely loved her and so did she. 'Well, there's nothing to be done about it,' snapped Gala. She would hear no more of her daughter's entreaties. 'Gala sometimes could be very hard,' Lidia observed.

It had been painful for Cécile to confront her mother; she was a melancholy teenager who reacted to the break between her parents by withdrawing deeper within herself. She was so shy – especially in the presence of her mother – that she usually whispered instead of speaking. Cécile was also plagued by a variety of sicknesses, some probably psychosomatic but others purely physical. Not long after the break-up of her parents' marriage, Cécile developed curvature of the spine.

In January 1932, Eluard and Gala's divorce was finalised.

When Dalí and Gala migrated back to Paris in the autumn of 1931, the art scene was slightly more receptive to him. An established gallery owner, Pierre Colle, organised a one-man exhibition for Dalí. The most compelling piece was *The Persistence of Memory*, which, with its soft watches, was to become an emblem not only for Dalí but of the entire surrealist movement. Dalí hit on the idea watching an oozy camembert cheese one night while Gala was at the cinema.

On her return, Dalí showed her the melting watches and asked: 'Do you think that in three years you will have forgotten this image?'

.'No one can forget it once he has seen it,' Gala replied.

Content, Dalí then asked Gala what film she had seen.

'I don't know . . . I can't remember it any more!'

Though Dalí's success was steadily growing, his bank balance was not. In 1933, when Dalí and Gala had moved into a modern studio on the rue Gauguet, a cul-de-sac where the nearby passing trains rattled the windows, Gala decided to take drastic action. Peddling Dalí's quirky inventions was not getting them anywhere. So she arranged a dinner with the Prince de Faucigny-Lucinge, the wealthy surrealist patron, at a restaurant near the Paris observatory. This time she left Dalí at home.

The prince recalled: 'They were hard up; she and Dalí were living in a place with two or three rooms. Gala said that, unless they got help, Dalí would have to commercialise his work.'

Quickly, Gala outlined her plan: the prince would club together some of his wealthy friends for a 'lottery'. Each member of the Zodiac – as the twelve collectors were to be called – would toss a yearly sum of 2500 francs into the pot for Dalí, and over a sumptuous dinner they would hold a draw, with the winner getting Dalí's newest work. Gala felt sure that the gambling ploy would grab the interest of the prince's rich acquaintances, and the prince agreed to her plan. He and his first recruit into the Zodiac, the Vicomte de Noailles, genuinely liked 'le petit Dalí' and appreciated his artistry. Others drawn into the circle were the writer Julien Green, the Marquise Cuevas de Vera and Caresse Crosby, the widow of an American banker.

The Prince de Faucigny-Lucinge was later to remark: 'The Zodiac group lasted until the war. Some of us ran into money troubles. And, of course, Dalí went to America. That's where he climbed to real fame – by commercialising himself.

Caresse Crosby provided more than money to Dalí and Gala; she was instrumental in persuading them to travel to the United States. They were introduced to her by René Crevel. Little caved-in 'Crevé', as he was called, with his tuberculosis, his drink and his unfashionable homosexuality, had helped Dalí and Gala immeasurably. For a communist, Crevel had some unexpectedly wealthy friends. One weekend in 1933, when Gala was still foraging for bargain vegetables in the market stalls, Crevel stopped by with a welcome diversion. Mrs Crosby, who owned the Black Sun Press, which published such expatriate luminaries as Ezra Pound, D. H. Lawrence and James Joyce, was holding one of her 'white lunches' and wanted a smattering of surrealists there.

Caresse Crosby, a tiny, energetic woman, lived in a château in the forest of Ermenonville near Paris; the interior of her château, Le Moulin du Soleil, was decorated entirely in white, and the guests drank milk. There were white walls and white rugs, and even she was clothed entirely in white. At Mrs Crosby's, Gala and Dalí heard Cole Porter's 'Night and Day' for the first time. The lustrous images of America inside *Town & Country* and *The New Yorker* magazines bewitched them. Luis Buñuel had gone to America, to Hollywood, the land of Buster Keaton and Harry Langdon, the two screen idols of the surrealists. Federico García Lorca, too, had sailed to New York and come away dazzled, with new poems that were strong and lyrical – not the sentimental gypsy romances that Dalí thought enfeebled Lorca's more recent work.

Cole Porter was not the only siren calling; there were the art collectors. In many ways, American museums and galleries were more susceptible to surrealism than was the mainstream European art world. The shock and razzmatazz of surrealism appealed to them. It was new, bizarre and free of the European cultural pretensions which many Americans find so daunting or infuriating. Explaining surrealism, *Life* magazine wrote later, in 1945, that 'most ordinary people have surrealist impulses – sudden inexplicable desires to punch their neighbours, draw mustaches on billboards or somehow make fools of themselves.' This made more sense to Americans than the theoretical principles of the movement as put forward by Breton.

Already, by 1931, Dalí's work had been seen in an exhibition in Pittsburgh and was included in the first surrealist show in America. This was not held in New York, oddly enough, but in a small and eclectic museum in Hartford, Connecticut, the Wadsworth Atheneum. Further, *The Persistence of Memory* had been bought by a shrewd young New York gallery owner, Julien Levy, for 'propaganda purposes', along with a few other Dalí paintings. Not all were sold but the exhibition attracted enough favourable reviews to encourage Levy to give Dalí a one-man show in 1933. Moreover, Europe was impoverished by depression, the American collectors had all the money, and Gala, perhaps more than Dalí, had lost patience with poverty.

The incentive to visit New York was strong. Levy could afford their passage, third-class, on a steamer but that was all. Somehow Gala and Dalí had to scrape up enough for the hotel. Dalí recounts how, for three days, he approached all his friends, even the remotest acquaintances, asking for money. Hard times had hit Paris, and Dalí and Gala were turned down by even their richest admirers. Yet eventually they succeeded in raising the money. It was only much later, in the 1950s, that Dalí overcame his pride and revealed the name of his mystery benefactor: Picasso.

10

The Persistence Of Money

On the transatlantic crossing on board the *Champlain*, Gala spent most of the voyage wearing a cork life-jacket, humouring Dalí. He was petrified. The thought of steaming across the Atlantic with only the thin metal skin of the ship between him and the deep water threw him into a panic. What if the ocean liner sank, he wondered. His paintings would be lost. Gala did her best to reassure him. She, after all, had sailed around the globe in search of Eluard and survived. He would not have sailed without Caresse Crosby on board to buoy up his courage.

Mrs Crosby occupied a higher, first-class berth, so again it was Gala who received the brunt of Dalí's paranoia. He dragged her along to every lifeboat drill and insisted that they parade around the deck in the emergency cork jackets. Dalí would even strap on the life-preserver while lounging around their cramped little cabin. 'I made Gala take the same interest as myself in all these annoying precautions, which either disgusted her or made her laugh till the tears rolled down her cheeks,' Dalí wrote of the crossing.

New York in 1934 was ready for someone like Dalí. The newspapers were filled with European madness of a more sinister kind: Hitler's continued rise to power in Germany. Now there was Dalí, a harmless eccentric, steaming past the Statue of Liberty like an intellectual travelling salesman who had arrived from Europe, his showcase stuffed with soft watches, tiny crutches for the drooping eyelids of aristocrats and other peculiar masterpieces. New York was in a party mood and this charming, chattering and quite incomprehensible Catalan was the perfect excuse for revelry. Prohibition had ended the year before, and the raucous blare of jazz saxophones seemed to sound from a thousand new clubs. After a decade of bathtub gin, New Yorkers were indulging in exotic cocktails and buying up aged whiskey and bourbon from pre-prohibitionary times. To someone coming from Europe, everything in New York would have seemed bigger, shinier and faster.

It was Caresse Crosby who directed the cameras towards Dalí and Gala. She was a celebrity – at one fancy-dress ball in Paris she had appeared on horseback as Lady Godiva – and after the ship docked in New York the newsmen soon swarmed around the pretty socialite with her two black whippets on a leash. When the photographers had finished snapping her, she sent them down to the third-class deck to find Dalí, who was in his cabin. The first sight of Dalí revealed a nervous little Spaniard with an eight-foot French loaf under his arm and at least a dozen paintings attached to himself with string. Dalí was afraid of thieves. New York, he had heard, was a rough place. With Mrs Crosby translating the titles, Dalí displayed his paintings. What caught the newsmen's attention was a realistic portrait of Gala with a pork chop on each shoulder like a general's epaulettes.

A great debate arose over the pork chops on Gala's shoulders. Were they raw or cooked? Did it matter? To Dalí it did. In his discourse to the gaping journalists who had crowded inside his third-class cabin, Dalí explained that of course they were more than mere pork chops. They represented his misplaced desire to cannibalise Gala. The journalists all looked at Gala, silent and very Russian, standing behind Dalí: she did not look very appetising. It was healthier to eat the pork chops, Dalí said, even though they were raw. Flashbulbs popped and the newsmen rushed off to Manhattan to report on the mad artist with the moustache and his inedible companion.

From that moment on, it became impossible to see Gala for the pork chops. Although Dalí exhibited all the subtlety of a three-ring circus, Gala was his opposite in that respect. In public, she was his product. Gala was as much of his art as the limp watches and the crutches. It is true that she nagged and dominated him, dressed him and practically tied his shoelaces. She handled business, set the prices and eagerly counted the money. But she was more than that to him. Gala fused herself to Dalí. While Dalí painted, Gala would sit beside him, reading aloud literature, philosophy and mythology. She never touched a brush, but Dalí insisted on signing each work with her name as well as his. He decorated their conjoined signature with a crown or wrote it in a long and stately manner as though he were a Francisco de Goya y Lucientes.

Gala was his critic too. She understood his art and would argue over the theme and content of a painting. With each painting, after Dalí had laid out the geometric guidelines and began sketching in his subjects, he would invite in the servants and the fishermen and ask them what they saw in the canvas. After the procession had finished, Gala would speak her opinion, which quite often was harsh. Sometimes Dalí listened, but just as often he grew angry and stubbornly resisted her suggestions, arguing that it was he, after all, who was the artist. When this happened, Gala invariably stormed from the studio. Their quarrels usually ended several hours later, according to one witness, Catalina Romans, with Dalí shouting out: ' "Olive" – he called her that – "come and give me a hug." And she would, too. A hug for her Daris, that was her pet name for him.'

Gala gave her past over to Dalí; she became his fiction, his secret. Anyone who dared pry into any aspect of her private life - even as innocent a question as how, as a young woman, she had fled Russia to reunite with Eluard – was slapped down with a curt 'None of your business'. Her secrecy was calculated to enhance their surrealist mystique. As Dalí once explained cryptically: 'Gala had the secret of remaining within my secret. Often people thought they had discovered my secret, but this was impossible, because it was not my secret but Gala's.'

This game of obfuscation served a dual purpose: not only did it add lustre to the modern myth of the artistic genius and his muse, but it also shielded them from outside intrusion into two sordid and painful incidents in their lives – Dalí's banishment from his family and Gala's disregard for her sickly daughter.

Dalí was plagued by insecurities, and Gala also learned to be his greatest champion. When an American interviewer asked who was the greatest artist alive today, Dalí hesitated, then finally replied:

'To your question, Picasso.'

'And then?'

'Then, Giorgio de Chirico.'

'And next?'

'After that, they all come together.'

The interviewer was curious to know where Dalí ranked

himself. He turned to Gala. 'So we do not embarrass anyone, how do you place Mr Dalí?'

'He is the very first, the greatest of all,' she said.

'I agree,' snapped Dalí.

Gala was not an exhibitionist – that aspect she left to Dalí – but she lived up to her part of the myth. Even in a crowded reception, she never passed unnoticed. Bettina Bergery recalls attending one reception with Gala and Dalí: 'It was jammed with people, but I could feel the presence of someone in the background. When I turned around, I saw that, of course, it was Gala. She had surrounded herself with young, handsome men.'

If Gala was not an exhibitionist, there was, however, one time during their first visit to New York when she unwittingly found herself at the centre of a furious scandal. On their last night in America Mrs Crosby threw a farewell party for them, the first surrealist ball ever held in America. The guests were a potent mixture of art gallery owners and high-society people, friends of Mrs Crosby, who took a crash course in surrealism to find out what these soft watches and pork chops were all about. The socialites were fast learners. The macabre costumes they dreamed up for this fancy-dress ball astonished even Dalí. Respectable society women, whose lives usually revolved around charity functions, turned up at the Coq Rouge restaurant wearing bird-cages around their heads and little else. The carcass of a cow hung from the ceiling stuffed with record players, in between a chunk of melting ice and a bathtub that threatened to tip over and douse everyone with water.

By comparison to the outlandish creations of the New York belles with their birdcages and eyeballs everywhere, Gala and Dalí's costumes seemed downright prudish. He went with a glass chest attached to his midriff containing a woman's brassière. As for Gala, Dalí dressed her as an 'Exquisite Corpse', from the surrealist parlour game of the same name. On her head was perched a doll, crawling with ants, whose head was being squeezed by a phosphorescent lobster. It seemed uncontroversial enough, but at the time New York was reeling from the trial of Bruno Hauptmann for the kidnap and murder of Charles Lindbergh's baby. A French journalist in New York, scraping for a story, suggested that Gala's baby resembled the Lindberghs' dead child and the uproar was unleashed. Dalí and Gala had barely heard of the Lindbergh baby and certainly didn't intend to work the grisly crime into a costume motif. Their dealer, Julien Levy, explained to them that, although a dash of artistic scandal never hurt, this was different. It was just the kind of sordid press attention that could have instantly killed off Dalí's rapid success in America.

Their first visit to the USA lasted only a few weeks, but Dalí and Gala had earned more publicity and more money than was possible in Paris. Even after Levy had scooped up his 50 per cent commission, a sizeable sum was still left. Gala adopted the habit of demanding to be paid either in cash – dollars preferably – or with a money order. Too many cheques in the past had bounced; too many dealers had gone bust. Later, Gala learned a trick over the telephone once a line was installed at Port Lligat. She would agree verbally to a price in pesetas and then pretend that she had made the deal in dollars. At that time, one dollar was worth many pesetas.

Meanwhile, the daily press publicity was matched by the keen curiosity of the art establishment in New York and Chicago. Among the cognoscenti, Dalí was already well-known. His unsellable 'propaganda piece', as Levy called *The Persistence of Memory*, had been bought by the Museum of Modern Art in 1932 and made a great impact. His one-man show at the Levy Gallery in 1933 had been a success. A second show, also a triumph, followed in New York the next year. Long after he and Gala sailed back across the Atlantic, the American public would continue hearing about Dalí. In 1936 the Museum of Modern Art mounted an impressive exhibition on Surrealism or the Art of the Marvellous and Fantastic. *The Persistence of Memory*, no bigger than a sheet of typewriter paper, was chosen as the showpiece. Because of this soft-watch painting and the flash of publicity, Dalí had received on his 1934 visit to New York, *Time* magazine chose Dalí for its cover story on surrealism. Man Ray, the American photographer and artist transplanted to Paris, shot *Time*'s December 1936 cover photo, portraying Dalí as a rather sinister figure, a dapper devil with a cinema actor's moustache. Suddenly Dalí was famous. His paintings soared in value. It became the risqué fad among very rich Americans to have their portrait done by Dalí, even if the results were shocking.

Dalí had sailed back to Europe in 1934 with a secret intact. He had persuaded the Americans that he was surrealism's leader, even though the Paris group had nearly expelled him.

11

A Premonition Of Boiled Beans

Just before his first New York visit, Dalí had been forced to kneel before Breton to avoid being banished from the surrealist group. One of his paintings, *The Enigma of William Tell*, depicted Lenin crouched and naked, with one flabby, elongated buttock. The surrealists were outraged – Lenin was their hero. The painting, on exhibition at the Grand Palais, so incensed Breton that he rounded up Tanguy and Péret and together they tried to slash holes in the Dalí canvas.

The next day, 5 February 1934, Dalí was summoned before a surrealist 'tribunal'. At this inquisition, Dalí's clownish antics are credited with having saved him from expulsion as a 'counter-revolutionary'. In a fever, Dalí arrived with a thermometer stuck in the corner of his mouth and many layers of clothes which he proceeded to peel off during Breton's harangue. Gala was not present at Breton's studio in the rue Fontaine. Breton had no wish to face an adversary as fierce as Gala in a public show-down. It was 'Invitation Only', with those in attendance openly hostile to Dalí for his shameless pursuit of publicity. As well as mocking Lenin, he had made a few careless remarks praising Hitler.

With his usual cunning, Breton waited until Eluard and Crevel had left town before summoning Dalí. He knew they would oppose Dalí's expulsion. Gala, however, hoping to marshal important allies, tracked them down in Nice and sounded the alarm. She had warned Dalí that the surrealists could be as rigid as a religious order but he had not listened. He had nursed hopes of dethroning Breton; being cast out had never occurred to him. Dalí liked being liked.

Train connections made it impossible for Eluard to rush back from Nice, but he wrote to Breton, arguing that Dalí's expulsion would split the group and deprive it of a masterful practitioner. Crevel also rallied round, as did Tristan Tzara, the rehabilitated Dadaist who had once suffered from Breton's intolerance. At the same time, Eluard advised Dalí through Gala to tone down his Hitlerian fantasies. The surrealists, Dalí once said, 'were the only ones who could say nice things' about Hitler. At this time, the Nazi Chancellor was extending his power through assassination and the persecution of communists, trade unionists and any politician who dared stand up to his Storm-troopers.

Nevertheless, Eluard's advice was not well taken. Gala bristled at the well-intended criticism of Dalí. She did not permit Eluard, Breton or anyone else to challenge his ideas, however frivolous and mercurial they might be. By trying to be diplomatic, Eluard ended up incurring the anger of both Gala and Breton. Dalí was far more malleable than Gala. At the surrealist tribunal, he left Breton grinding his green pipe between his teeth in a rage by first expressing his right to paint himself sodomising Breton, and then dropping to his knees and swearing that he was not an 'enemy of the proletariat'. All the hostile surrealists guffawed at this scene, which Dalí acted out with the thermometer still jammed in his mouth, and Breton had to relent. Dalí's excommunication was postponed until 1948 – by which time Breton's condemnation no longer mattered to him, since his high-priced paintings were being bought by the best American museums.

However, this near-expulsion in 1934 affected Dalí and Gala as a couple. They coiled in on themselves. Even Gala's letters to Eluard grew sparse. In one touching note, Eluard remarked that he had begun to see in Cécile, then sixteen, much of Gala, the 'nervous girl, pure and pathetic, that you have always been for me'. Gala and Eluard's fortunes had also reversed. With his inheritance drained away by Cécile's medical bills and losses on the Paris stock exchange, Eluard was forced to borrow money from Gala. She loaned him some, but not much; it was paltry compared to the amount that she had taken from him to sustain her early romance with Dalí.

On their return from America in 1934, Gala and Dalí retreated to Port Lligat. Their fishing hut had grown into a comfortable home. They bought up the stone huts next door and connected them with a labyrinth of stairways. They scaled away the layers of slate behind the house and laid down a terrace where they could devour their sea urchins raw in the shade of an olive tree

91

and look out over the inlet of Port Lligat. Once the procession of white and blue fishing boats filed out of the port, Gala and Dalí were entirely alone and they found their solitude delicious. Often Gala would read poetry, philosophy or scientific tomes out loud to Dalí as he painted.

Meanwhile, the feud between Dalí and his father had eased, slightly. Some of the misgivings that Dalí's father had about the unsavoury relationship between his son and Gala were calmed when the couple were married in a civil ceremony on 30 January 1934. It was, for Dalí, an uncharacteristically quiet affair, one that Gala had talked him into at Eluard's suggestion. The reasons for the marriage were more practical than emotional. Under Spanish law, Gala stood to lose all of Dalí's wealth – and much of her own – if he died or went insane. Eluard, who had finally divorced Gala two years before, was not opposed to the marriage. It freed him to pursue his frail Nusch, though he still made love to Gala whenever the opportunity arose, as it often did.

Even inside the seclusion of their stone maze in Port Lligat, Dalí and Gala were shaken by the political turbulences of Spain. Dalí was not a fascist; he had adopted this posture to provoke the left-wing surrealists. He was the first to admit that his cowardice, his absolute terror over the 'slightest material worry', as Breton once observed, precluded any ideological stand. Gala's apoliticism was more profound. She had seen how the Russian Revolution had ravaged her family, brought famine and hardship. Gala had used every strategy, every wile and threat, to keep Eluard from the trenches of the Somme, and she was not about to let Dalí become embroiled in the fanatic currents of anarchism, separatism, communism and fascism sweeping through Catalonia.

With disastrously bad timing, they chose to leave for Barcelona just as the Catalonian politicians were on the verge of breaking away from Spain to form an independent state. The city was paralysed by a general strike; the bourgeoisie had the good sense to disguise themselves as factory workers; the flag of Catalonia and the anarchists' red and black banners hung from every big building. Dalí had been invited there to lecture by an art dealer, Dalmau. Whatever provocative topic Dalí had in mind for his lecture palled alongside the madness in Barcelona's streets.

Dalmau, in any event, had cancelled Dalí's lecture and advised him to flee across the French border before the Spanish army marched in to restore order. Dalmau was too busy making escape plans for his own family to help Dalí and Gala. The few words of Catalan slang that Gala had learned from her fishermen friends at Port Lligat were hardly enough to see her through the bureaucratic paperwork needed to obtain a swift exit visa. Gala was hardly a linguist; even her French, the language in which she and Dalí communicated, was appalling. For once, Dalí, who trembled at having to buy a tram ticket and who needed Gala to pin money to his jacket so he wouldn't lose it, was on his own. All Gala could do was hold his hand as they hastened towards the government ministry, past prowling groups of vigilantes. It took two hours for the visa because the civil servants, instead of typing, were mounting machine-guns at the windows.

Conspirators and secret police were everywhere. Gala, Dalí and Dalmau had to cram inside a men's toilet to meet with an anarchist taxi driver who was willing, for a considerable sum of money, to drive them into France. The trip was harrowing, with roadblocks every few kilometres along the road manned by rival militias. Once Gala and Dalí made the mistake of stopping in a seaside village. A gang of armed men saw Gala's many expensive suitcases, took her and Dalí to be decadent capitalists and wanted to shoot them. Their anarchist driver earned his colossal fee by talking the gang out of setting up an impromptu firing squad. After a detour to collect Dalí's paintings in Cadaqués, the driver delivered Gala and Dalí safely to France. The driver, though, never had a chance to spend his money. On the way back to Barcelona, he was killed by a stray bullet.

The uprising was crushed, but everyone hid their guns, waiting for the Civil War which came two years later. Once an illusory calm was restored in 1935 Dalí and Gala slipped back to Cadaqués. They were acompanied by Edward James, a diminutive English aristocrat whose mother may have been either the illegitimate daughter of Edward VII or the monarch's mistress. James was recovering from an ugly divorce from an Austrian ballerina, Tily Losch, who had married James thinking she was safe with a rich homosexual who would ignore her many affairs. However, she had underestimated her own seductive charms, for James immediately got her pregnant. She separated from him, and James responded in an ungentlemanly fashion by filing for divorce. James won, but the public humiliation tarred him. He left England to roam the continent, holding parties in palaces he had rented in Rome and Paris with his large inheritance. In Paris he dabbled in surrealism, wrote poetry and helped finance the famous magazine, *Minotaure*. James latched on instantly to Dalí. They might have been brothers; both were small in size, dapper and outrageous show-offs.

James told an interviewer, George Melly, many years later, that he and Dalí had made love together, and that Gala had become furious on discovering this. She had packed her bags and was about to storm out when James, at Dalí's suggestion, bribed her into staying by giving her an enormous art-nouveau jewel. Dalí never mentioned this affair, however, and close friends of James do not give it much credence.

It was while James was staying at Cadaqués that Dalí reforged his friendship with Federico García Lorca. Dalí and Lorca, the best of friends from student days in Madrid, had fallen out in 1928 over Dalí's harsh criticism of the poet's book, *Romancero Gitano*. The criticism must have wounded Lorca, for he never answered back. The poet may have had another reason for losing interest in Dalí: Gala.

Lorca had frequently tried to seduce Dalí during their student days together at the Madrid Residencia and during summer holidays at Cadaqués. Lorca was a handsome homosexual with an athletic build and the shining dark eyes of a Moor. Buñuel, who also happened to lodge at the Residencia, once described Lorca as 'the finest human being' he had ever met – 'He was like a flame.'

Did Lorca succeed in seducing Dalí? Almost, according to Dalí. Dalí told friends later that the poet wooed him into bed and a little further still. Sodomy was too painful for Dalí, and he and Lorca stopped halfway. Dalí claimed that afterwards he played a cruel practical joke on Lorca. When Lorca tried again to persuade Dalí to sleep with him, Dalí agreed and told Lorca to meet him in his room late at night. The lights were off when Lorca entered and slipped in to join whom he thought was Dalí in bed, but it did not take him long to realise that the naked body he was caressing belonged to a woman, a coarse prostitute, and Dalí was hidden somewhere in the dark room, laughing. García Lorca was furious.

That, anyway, is how Dalí told the story. Dalí's friends treated it with scepticism. 'Dalí was afraid of touching anyone. Physical contact of any kind terrorised him,' said one of the painter's female confidantes. There is no doubt, however, that Dalí's sexual confusion encouraged Lorca, but once Dalí was united with Gala that ambiguity was settled. Lorca's ardour, sensibly, waned.

Gala was curious about Lorca. Dalí had often spoken of him – his charm, his lyrical power as a poet, his feline attractiveness. Lorca was equally curious about Gala. Ian Gibson, Lorca's biographer, claims he confessed to Rafael Alberti, a communist poet and friend, that he 'could not conceive of any woman being capable of pleasing Dalí sexually, with his hatred of female breasts and genitals, his terror of coitus and his anal obsession. What woman could lend herself to participate in the erotic games of the painter, in his fantasies?'

Dalí too was eager for Lorca to meet Gala. It was as though he were seeking from the poet the blessing that had been denied by his own father. Edward James came to this reunion on the Tarragona coast, south of Barcelona, and one wonders if he were not encouraged along by Gala, who was jealous of anyone, male or female, becoming too intimate with Dalí. James, who vacillated between boy and girl bedmates, would have been the perfect distraction for García Lorca. The two men were attracted, but Lorca rather derisively described the tiny Englishman, who pranced about in Tyrolean lederhosen, as resembling a humming-bird dressed up like a soldier of Swift's day.

Lorca turned down James's invitation to join Gala and Dalí as his guests in Italy. Dalí was secretly relieved. He was writing an ode, entitled 'I eat Gala', and was jealous of Lorca's superior talent as a writer. Dalí's envy was to haunt him later on; García Lorca was murdered several months later in Granada by fascists, and Dalí cursed himself for not having coaxed Lorca into coming to Italy with them. There is no record of Lorca's impression of Gala, but she apparently did not disturb their old friendship. 'We are two twin spirits,' he wrote of himself and Dalí. 'Here is the proof: seven years without seeing each other and we've coincided in everything, as though we had been speaking every day.'

News of Lorca's killing reached the Dalís in Italy. So did other horror stories that jarred the normally self-obsessed Dalí into some semblance of moral anguish over what was happening in Spain. Over thirty fishermen in Cadaqués, all friends, were gunned down; anarchist soldiers in Vic, a town in Catalonia, played football with the archbishop's severed head. It was during this upheaval too that Dalí's sister, Ana Maria, was tortured by military intelligence agents. As outrage against Franco mounted among the Paris surrealists, pressure grew on Dalí to take a stand. Was he, after all, a fascist? Eluard and the others were beginning to wonder. His painting, *Soft Construction of Boiled Beans: Premonition of Civil War*, caught Spain's inner torment but it lacked political commitment at a time when intellectuals were entrenching themselves ideologically. Again, Gala dissuaded Dalí from taking sides.

In the meantime, Gala persuaded Edward James to buy everything that Dalí produced that year – for a huge sum. James could afford it, but like many wealthy men he grew suspicious of being cheated. It seems that Gala may have given in to the temptation of not giving James all of Dalí's output. She made plenty of trips up to Paris from Italy, and it was easy enough for her to sneak several small paintings into her suitcases and sell them in Paris. There was no shortage of buyers, visiting Americans who had read of Dalí's antics in their home newspapers. James never accused the Dalís directly but held a grudge against them until his death.

Edward James also had a tendency to regard plants and animals often more highly than humans, and he was appalled by Dalí and Gala's cruelty. Gala had an act of surrealistic purity that she would practise for shock effect wherever she stayed. She would buy a pet rabbit, give it a cuddly name, feed and pamper it for several months. Then, with no explanation or show of feeling, she would order the cook to slaughter the rabbit and serve it to her for lunch.

Gala and Dalí seemed to have an uncanny ability to dodge catastrophe. They had barely escaped death in the Catalonian uprising of 1934. They returned in 1935 to Cadaqués and just three months after their departure for Italy, Spain exploded in civil war. Lorca, whose behaviour and politics were no more aberrant than Dalí's, was assassinated. The same fate probably awaited Dalí and Gala had they remained in Cadaqués. Italy under Mussolini was becoming intolerable, even inside the frescoed palaces of Edward James. Nazi Germany had annexed Czechoslovakia and by 1939 was poised to invade Poland, a move that triggered the Second World War. France was readying itself for the inevitable moment when Hitler would turn his forces against the old enemy. Picasso, the contemporary artist most admired by Dalí, had painted *Guernica* after the Nazis bombed this Basque town on market day. Eluard, forty-three, had enlisted ('the oldest lieutenant in France', as he grimly referred to himself). Amidst this *danse macabre*, all that Dalí contemplated was where in France he could retire to paint and eat well. He settled on the town of Arcachon, near Bordeaux, because of its oysters. There Gala would also find another pet rabbit.

In 1939 they arrived in Arcachon, flush with dollars from New York, and took a fine rococo villa beside an ornamental lake. Dalí had been scandalously successful in America. He had landed himself in the front-page headlines again – by being arrested. The large New York department store, Bonwit Teller, had commissioned him to design two window displays. Dalí and Gala had worked through the night, lining an old bathtub with black lambswool, filling it with water and floating a few wax arms holding mirrors in the mess.

They slept in late, and then strolled down Fifth Avenue the next afternoon, curious about New Yorkers' reactions to the display. It seems the store had so many complaints from window-shoppers that Dalí's artwork was censored in his absence. A robe was draped around the mannequin stepping into the tub. Dalí was enraged. He sent Gala back to the hotel, to call for reinforcements. Then he stormed into the window display, knocking the tub through the window and, somehow, the next moment stepping out on to the pavement in between sheets of falling glass. A passing detective immediately arrested him on a charge of malicious mischief. Gala arrived minutes later, 'spitting mad, ready to scratch anyone's eyes out', according to Julien Levy, who had answered Gala's urgent summons. Gala followed the police wagon down to the East 51st Street station and sat meekly with him on the bench, eating tinned pears and milk. The night-court judge, more accustomed to gangsters and thieves, suspended Dalí's sentence because, he opined, 'These are some of the privileges that an artist with temperament seems to enjoy.'

Arcachon was a *fin de siècle* resort much in vogue with Parisian writers and actors, built around a tidal basin whose mud was said to contain curative minerals as well as oysters. Dalí painted demonically, immersing himself in the alchemy of amber oils, paint and varnish as if he were seeking some chemical combination that could transform the madness of Europe's war, and its invasion of his own psyche, more exactly on to canvas. Picasso's Guernican horses and people were splintered in agony; Dalí's response was intellectual. For him, the war was not a struggle of good versus evil or of geo-political imperatives. Instead, Dalí saw it as tradition trying to reassert itself against the 'deficiencies, nothingnesses and revolutions of our sceptical, formless . . . epoch'. As he painted, Gala read him books on science, philosophy, metaphysics, architecture – anything that could give him a vision of the world that lay beyond the darkness of war.

Gala too became obsessed with the future. If she could, she would not let the Nazis catch Dalí and her unaware. Living with Eluard, when the surrealists were experimenting with seances, automatic writing and spiritualism, Gala found she had an affinity for the tarot. There in Arcachon, she spent hours reading the cards. No matter how she shuffled them, the same trump cards kept turning up: the Hangman, an upside-down youth with gold coins spilling from his pockets, the horned Devil and the skeleton of Death, scything its own leg, and the people rising from the earth. Would war descend on France? And when? Again and again, Gala consulted the cards, and the ominous sequence of Devil, Hangman and Death would appear always. Gala's ability in reading the cards was uncanny; according to Dalí, she foretold the very day of Hitler's invasion of France and the suicide of René Crevel.

They had their visitors. Dalí did not choose Arcachon just for the food; the jolt of publicity he had received in America required some recharging and Arcachon had a few summer celebrities with whom he enjoyed mingling. The Dalís renewed their friendship with the artist Marcel Duchamp and the fashion designer Coco Chanel. New York art collectors had emptied their wallets for Dalí. For an artist, he was rich, but that did not stop Gala from badgering Chanel to give her gowns at bargain prices or, preferably, for free. Gala would wear these creations until they literally disintegrated, twenty years later.

In the villa next to the Dalís there lived Léonor Fini, a beautiful Argentine woman once described as 'a painter of perverse enchantments'. They had met several times before at Parisian parties but had never spoken much. What instantly attracted Gala to her new neighbour was the huge American automobile parked in the driveway of her villa. It belonged to one of Léonor's houseguests. 'Gala reproached me for this somehow,' said Léonor, 'because they didn't have one. Gala thought the car could have been useful to them.' Gala's arrogance amused Léonor. 'She was very lively, intelligent, well informed but not "intellectual". She was concrete, swift and ready to laugh. Usually she kept her small mouth shut very tight. The only time she would open her tiny mouth wide would be with a derisive laugh or, more rarely, with instant amusement.'

Léonor Fini often painted women, naked lost women in swamps, and she took an artistic interest in Gala, who was then in her early forties. 'I could understand why she was considered "physically" attractive. She was small but well proportioned, her skin was sombre – close to a leathery colour – and her eyes were very near together but they weren't narrow. They were very small, very black, very attentive and on a slant across her face. She had a well-designed nose, I must say, strong of form and precise. Her hair was glossy black and fine, always close to her head.' This mid-life portrait of Gala is best summed up with Léonor's impression of her hands: they were sensual but tightly clasped. She also noted that Gala's walk was sure, manly.

While Dalí painted, Gala often wandered over to Léonor's villa. Gala would question her on technique, how she obtained the smooth surface of her canvases. It might have been genuine curiosity, but more probably Dalí sent her to spy on Léonor's work. Having dismissed all women as bad painters, Dalí was probably too arrogant to admit that he could learn a few pointers. Gala did not share Dalí's prejudices. Once she offered Léonor to 'take care of her, too' as a kind of agent. 'I'd never accept it,' said Léonor, who none the less took the proposal as real praise. 'Gala never flattered anyone.'

What impressed Léonor was Gala's idea that 'every instant of life had to represent a revenge, a conquest, or an advantage'. She was, however, repulsed by the same thing that had bothered Edward James: their cruelty to animals. They gloried in this cruelty, with Dalí telling tales of how, as a child, he once sawed off the beak of a pelican so it would starve to death. Gala, inevitably, invited Léonor over to the banquet serving her pet rabbit. 'As best I could, I tried to keep from showing my horror,' said Léonor, 'because that would have stimulated their sadism.' Gala also began collecting flies. It was an easy task, for Dalí seldom bathed or changed his food-stained shirt.

The radio carried the latest grim news from the battlefields. By May 1940 the Germans had captured Holland, Belgium and Luxembourg. By late May the Nazis had cut through the French defences, and by 14 June the German army was marching past the Arc de Triomphe. But until that day, there, beside the small, misty lake at Arcachon, the war seemed forgotten.

Gala and the two artists felt as though they were on an 'untouchable islet'. This illusion was abruptly shattered by the swarm of refugees fleeing from Paris. 'A very anguished friend came from Paris crying that the Germans had gunned down "everybody",' said Léonor. 'The Dalís left immediately, in their nightrobes, leaving behind everything. Their canvases and suitcases were shipped after. Dalí was absolutely terrified.'

Dalí persuaded Gala to return to Paris to secure the paintings left behind in their flat before they fled to America. There was no question of Dalí going himself. If recognised, he would be immediately arrested by the Gestapo. The Germans were unlikely to appreciate his fascination with Hitler. Friends like Dalí the Third Reich did not need; the Nazi view of surrealism was that its followers should be locked in insane asylums and sterilised to stop their subversive ideas from infecting another generation.

Gala, on the other hand, carried a French passport and could slip into Paris more easily. The only foreseeable problem was her Slavic features. The Nazis might think she was a Jewess. The trains arriving in Bordeaux were crammed with Jewish families who feared, with good reason, that the Nazi persecution of Jews in Germany and Poland would repeat itself in France. The Dalís needed Spanish visas from the consulate in Bordeaux to cross into Portugal and, from there, sail over to America.

Every instinct must have warned Gala to turn back. Her train compartment was empty, and as she rattled along she could see burning factories, squadrons of Stukas and Messerschmitts droning overhead to destroy the fleeing remnants of the French army. The retreating soldiers she saw were miserable, their faces deformed by fatigue, grimy and wounded. She must have wondered about Eluard, France's 'oldest lieutenant'. Had he been killed, taken prisoner along with half a million other Frenchmen? The trains coming from Paris were so stuffed with refugees that those who could not find places on board rode clinging to the wagons. It made Gala's train seem emptier. The exodus on the roads was even more frightening for someone heading against the current of terror, towards the big boom of the artillery guns and the flames. Petrol was scarce, and Parisians fled on foot, on bicycles and even on the donkey carts from Les Halles vegetable market. All were trudging towards the ever-shrinking portion of unoccupied France, camping in the fields and forests along the road when exhaustion overtook them.

The Nazis had not bombed Paris. The city was intact, empty of all but Teutonic conquerors turned tourists, snapping photographs of themselves beside the Arc de Triomphe and Napoleon's tomb. A few cafés were open. Maxim's restaurant, which had served foie gras to a few intrepid diners while Nazi tanks rolled up the Champs-Elysées, had finally drawn down the shades. From friends, Gala learned Eluard was safe. The army had made him a quartermaster at a warehouse in the Loiret, and Nusch was with him, living in a hotel near the barracks. Pursued by the Gestapo, Eluard and Nusch later took refuge in an insane asylum run by a doctor who was a member of the resistance.

The next step for Gala was to reach Portugal. Spain under Franco was officially neutral, but sympathetic to the Germans. The consul's wife at Bordeaux had all her family executed by Loyalists – the losers of the Civil War – and sought her revenge on any suspicious Spaniard and spouse. Dalí and Gala fitted the bill. The consulate was stormed several times by angry refugees, and people were paying 10,000 francs just to have their suitcases delivered across the border. The hire of a fishing boat to sail across the Cantabrian Sea to Portugal ran to 250,000 francs.

Dalí left Arcachon on his own. Before leaving for Lisbon, where he had arranged to rendezvous with Gala, Dalí made a detour over to Figueras. The welfare of his father and sister concerned him. The entire province of Gerona had been ravaged by the Civil War, and Dalí had heard that Figueras, in particular, had been hit hard by marauding armies of both Loyalist and Republican forces. His father was so relieved at seeing Dalí that he immediately forgave him for everything. The curse was lifted, the boy reprieved.

He was welcomed home, but Dalí was no doubt glad that Gala had not joined him. It seems that Ana Maria, who had been tortured by military inquisitors, blamed Gala for having disclosed false information that set the torturers on her trail. This accusation seems implausible: Gala had not been in Spain since 1935, and most of her time before that had been spent with Dalí in

Cadaqués, far from the Barcelona headquarters of the Military Intelligence Committee. Although Ana Maria refused to be interviewed about Gala, close friends and relatives said she never supported this charge with any proof. She apparently cracked under interrogation and was released after two days. Even when Dalí visited Figueras *en route* to Lisbon, she had still not recovered completely. Most likely, Ana Maria deluded herself into believing that Gala, having severed the close bond between brother and sister, wanted to complete the destruction of her rival. She was especially jealous of Dalí; perhaps she even sensed Dalí's undeniably incestuous feelings towards her. One of Dalí's adolescent attempts at poetry celebrated the beauty of his sister's sphincter.

Meanwhile, as the Nazi troops swept across France, Gala's daughter was trying in vain to reunite with her mother. Cécile had been working as a secretary for the government wheat office when she was transferred out of Paris ahead of the German invasion. All employees of this strategically vital department were transported by coach to southern France. Cécile's coach reached the river Loire, only to be commandeered by retreating French soldiers, and Cécile had no choice but to hitchhike south. 'I took to the road,' she later recalled. 'All I had was one suitcase and two months' wages saved from my very modest job.' By the time Cécile finally arrived in Arcachon, Gala had returned from Paris and departed for Lisbon. 'The woman who worked as my mother's servant told me that she had never known Madame Dalí had a daughter. I had to insist that she did have a daughter, and that was me.' Fortunately, Cécile was able to enlist the help of Marcel Duchamp, who persuaded the maid that Cécile was indeed Gala's child.

Even if Cécile had arrived at Arcachon earlier, it is doubtful that she would have wanted to accompany the Dalís on their passage to the United States. It is also doubtful that Gala would have wanted the burden of this filial baggage. Cécile must have felt that, no matter how desperately she sought her mother's affection and approval, it was always being withheld. When Gala corresponded, she did so out of duty; Eluard was always chiding Gala to write to her daughter. Mother and daughter were further estranged by Cécile's impulsive marriage, at the age of twenty-two, to the writer Luc Décaunes, who was taken prisoner by the Germans early in the war. Both Gala and Eluard disapproved of Cécile's choice, and that wounded her. In all likelihood, Cécile did not want to escape France – even if Gala had offered to take her. Duchamp gave her lodging in Arcachon for a while; he craved a chess partner. After several weeks, she drifted back to Paris and eventually made postal contact with her mother. Cécile's paltry savings had been used up; she begged her mother for help. Paris during the occupation was grim. Jobs were scarce, as were food and fuel. Gala had money but could not send it. The United States and Germany were at war. What she could do, though, was let Cécile use the Dalís' flat in Paris.

This was to damage their relationship irrevocably. When Gala and Dalí returned after the war, many of Dalí's canvases and much furniture were missing from the flat. Gala accused Cécile of selling their possessions and, for that, she never forgave her daughter.

12

The Surrealist In Hollywood

When they docked in New York on 16 August 1940 Dalí did not need to bake any eight-foot-long bread this time to gain publicity. He was assured press coverage galore after the Bonwit Teller scandal. America was ripe for surrealism. During the 1930s and 1940s its influence pervaded billboard advertisements; furniture grew shapely female legs, painted eyes blinked from watch faces, a surrealist dream had become obligatory in Hollywood suspense films and even the Marx Brothers cracked surrealist jokes. Surrealism helped sell Ford cars and chewing gum. Other painters of the movement may have been more acclaimed – René Magritte or Max Ernst, for example – but Dalí happily waxed his moustache, twirled his cane and became surrealism personified. Back in Paris, the other surrealists, outraged at his success, had nicknamed him derisively 'Avida Dollars' – Breton's bitchy anagram for Salvador Dalí – but that bit of news never mattered to the Americans. They wanted fun, to be entertained and startled. Against Dalí's clowning, the stony sedition of Breton never stood a chance in the USA. All Gala did was set the price tag.

Gala did indeed push Dalí into commercialism, and the quality of his work undoubtedly suffered for it. Would Dalí have been a more honest artist without her? Without Gala, Dalí would probably not have been in any condition to paint. She saved him from madness once, in 1929, but having his picture on the cover of *Time* magazine was no insurance against Dalí falling victim to his paranoia again. Every day was rife with crises, a minefield that Dalí could negotiate only by rearranging his immediate reality, surrounding himself in a small but exquisite airtight bubble. Lots of money was needed to maintain this bubble, more than Dalí could earn if he restricted himself to only creating his precise masterpieces. In his mind, Dalí was always able to differentiate between his assembly-line art and the serious work over which he agonised. He was also able to justify his careless mass production of lithographs, doodles commissioned by magazines for extravagant sums and his advertising work as a kind of surrealistic subversion; the silly bourgeoisie (a term from which Dalí would recoil) were paying him handsomely to make fools of them.

Dalí loved playing this game of 'cretinising' his admirers. He delighted in ridiculing his devotees by persuading them that some idiocy or other was high art. One wonders whether Gala's imperiousness was her own version of the game, whether she and Dalí shared a laugh over how these grand socialites could be coaxed into emptying their wallets or being made to perform the most slavish duties. Although her shell was harder than that of Dalí's telephone lobster, Gala undoubtedly felt insecure about herself – and Dalí – amid these rich strangers. Her tyranny was a means of justifying her own behaviour by getting others to mould their lives around Dalí's whims just as she had.

Dalí's sell-out was also due to Gala's avarice. Her fear of poverty drove away whatever qualms Dalí may have had about turning out rubbish. She pushed him hard, the way a mother would with a lazy son unwilling to do household chores. Friends say that as soon as Gala left his studio Dalí would drop his palette and brushes with relief; then, as soon as he heard Gala's returning footsteps, Dalí would swiftly pretend to be hard at work. He feared her scoldings. The simple reason for his commercialism, however, was that in the United States there was an irresistible demand for anything that Dalí produced.

The press were primed for an event similar to the Bonwit Teller scandal of 1939, but this time Dalí was more subdued. Their flight from the German invasion and the scramble in Lisbon to find a berth on an America-bound ship had exhausted them. After recuperating for several days, he and Gala travelled by train down to Caresse Crosby's estate, Hampton Manor, near Fredericksburg, Virginia, where they would spend the winter.

Dalí's relations with the American press were curious. Although the reporters viewed him as an astute self-aggrandiser, he was redeemed, in their eyes, by his genuine eccentricity. The more perceptive interviewers noted that, for all his artistic pyrotechnics, Dalí had no close friends and that he and Gala wrapped themselves in the same cocoon. An article in *Life* magazine commented that Dalí had 'virtually no friends' and added: 'The people who surround him are either patrons of his art or curious onlookers who treat him like a strange animal in a zoo. Despite a decade of the most assiduous self-advertisement, Dalí has apparently succeeded in disclosing his real self to only one person – his wife, Gala.'

It was in Gala's interests that no one should get as close to Dalí as she had; she was jealous not only of other women but also of other men, the writers and artists who tried to become his spiritual companions. As one Catalan acquaintance remarked: 'Dalí had a habit of becoming entranced with people – usually for no more than four days. It could be because of the colour of your hair, or something humorous you might have said. Gala would cut these people off – sharply. She could be unspeakably obnoxious.' Long-time acquaintances say that Gala also had an annoying habit of wanting the world to worship Dalí's genius as much as she did. Any doubt shown by friends was akin to treason. Reynolds Morse, a collector who with his wife, Eleanor, knew Gala and Dalí for over thirty years, was once bawled out by Gala. 'How dare you criticise Dalí!' she shouted. 'How dare you be so ungrateful. I don't understand why you don't get down on your knees in front of the Maestro the way Picasso's collectors do with him.'

The most telling account of Gala's zealousness relates to the winter of 1940 at Caresse Crosby's estate in Fredericksburg, where Dalí and Gala took refuge, as paying guests. According to the writer Anaïs Nin, who was also a guest there and who first met them at breakfast after they arrived:

Both small in stature, they sat close together. Both were unremarkable in appearance, she all in moderate tones, a little faded, and he drawn with charcoal like a child's drawing of a Spaniard, any Spaniard, except for the incredible length of his moustache. They turned towards each other as if for protection, reassurance, not open, trusting or at ease. . . . Was Dalí truly mad? Was it a pose? Was his a spontaneous eccentricity or calculated?.

[Mrs Crosby and her other guests] wanted me to solve this riddle because I could speak Spanish, but they had not foreseen the organisational powers of Mrs Dalí. Before we were even conscious of it, the household was functioning for the well-being of Dalí. We were not allowed to enter the library because he was going to work there. Would Dudley mind driving to Richmond and trying to find odds and ends which Dalí needed for his painting? Would I mind translating an article for him? Would Caresse invite *Life* magazine to come and visit?

So we each fulfilled our appointed tasks. Mrs Dalí never raised her voice, never seduced or charmed. Quietly she assumed we were all there to serve Dalí, the great, indisputable genius.

Anaïs Nin made the effort of cooking a Spanish meal for Dalí and Gala but it was a flop. 'Madame Dalí did not appreciate Spanish cooking,' commented Anaïs Nin tartly. Rebellion among the guests was never contemplated, at least for several months, during which time Gala enlisted the help of Mrs Crosby in typing up Dalí's autobiography, *A Secret Life*, while Gala herself organised the scribbles that Dalí handed her. When a *Life* magazine photographer eventually turned up, Mrs Crosby gamely followed Dalí's instructions to herd a cow into the library and suspend a grand piano from a tree on the snowy lawn. According to a visitor from *The New Yorker*, Dalí spent most of his time cooped up painting while he listened to the radio or sang homesick songs of Spain. Gala too was housebound and ended up driving everyone crazy.

Their sole entertainment was playing chess. A newspaperman who visited the Crosby mansion reported that Dalí's method of play was suitably surrealistic: 'Usually he moves his king all over the board until his opponent, disarmed by the confusion, makes a grave mistake or the king falls into a fatal trap.' Gala, his habitual adversary, never made an error and always beat him.

Dalí's autobiography tells much of his worship for Gala's every orifice, but is remarkable for the little it reveals of Gala's character. As Dalí's biographer, Meryle Secrest, writes: 'There is a puzzlingly abstract quality to the love [Dalí's for Gala] so vaunted, as there is a distinct coldness at the very core of the book, a kind of chilly detachment, as if he were observing himself observing himself in an infinity of mirrors.'

A few months after Anaïs Nin's first visit to Hampton Manor, she stopped there again. By this time Gala's commandeering manner was grating on all the guests. She demanded that they speak French at the table, even though Gala's English by then was good enough for her to translate for Dalí on their lecture tours around the USA. Dalí was a finicky eater and the other guests had to cater to his tastes. He abhorred minced meat and seldom ate anything other than shellfish, day after day. This proved too much even for the affable Mrs Crosby, and by the time Dalí and Gala left for the west coast their friendship was irreparably damaged.

Hollywood was a lure that Dalí could not resist. There he painted portraits of film moguls, actresses and actors, often charging up to $25,000. Alfred Hitchcock, the film director, consulted with Dalí before shooting his dream sequence in *Spellbound*. The maître d's at Romanoff's and the Brown Derby always showed him and Gala to their best tables. Harpo Marx posed with Dalí, and even Greta Garbo was coaxed out of her seclusion. Through a mutual friend Dalí arranged for Garbo to join him for afternoon tea at the Hollywood cottage that he and Gala rented. Garbo was Dalí's favourite actress, and he looked forward to her visit with near hysteria. He decided to dress himself up as a suave film star. Hours before the appointed time, the nervous Dalí had already pomaded his hair and waxed his moustache, and, after agonising over his outfit, he finally selected a shimmering satin suit which he wore with a starched shirt and tie.

Garbo came late as usual, wearing men's chinos and tennis shoes. She took one look at Dalí and said: 'One of us has got this wrong. Why don't we try again?' She kissed Dalí full on the lips and departed without another word. Dalí was stunned into speechlessness; he hated being kissed on the mouth, even by Garbo. They never met again.

Having amassed many commissions, it was time for Dalí to paint. He and Gala rented a bungalow on the sea cliffs of Monterey, battered by the wind and waves into shapes similar to those of the rocks at Port Lligat. For the many tourists and admirers who tracked them down in the Del Monte Lodge, expecting a Taj Mahal of strangeness, the Dalí dwelling was a disappointment. Built from California redwoods, and decorated with plain, Sears-Catalogue-type furniture, their home, as one reporter described it, resembled a 'luxurious tourist cabin'. Dalí dressed the part, wearing an embroidered cowboy shirt, moccasins and a frontiersman leather jacket. 'Among strangers,' said a *Life* magazine reporter, 'he claims to speak no English except the word "Connecticut" which he learned because he likes the sound of it. Actually Dalí understands enough English to read his press clippings, which he hoards jealously and pores over with intense satisfaction.'

Gala was no less adept at projecting the proper press image of muse, mother and minder. Of Gala, *Life* wrote, 'she is self-effacing, shrewd and practical. . . . She pays the bills, signs the contracts and otherwise acts as a buffer between Dalí and the world of reality. When he goes out on an errand, she carefully ties a tag to his clothing with his destination plainly written on it so that he will not get lost.'

In America, Dalí was even more helpless than usual. Gala too, for all her strength and adaptability, must have found herself lost in this new continent, without knowing its language or its rough and puritanical customs. It was bearable when they were in New York and Hollywood among friends; in Monterey, however, they lived reclusively.

Gala grew restless. She needed to escape from Dalí, to restore herself from his exhausting demands. In Monterey she sought solitude the American way: she drove. After dropping Dalí off at his white, arched studio several miles from Del Monte Lodge, she would speed to and fro in her Cadillac, up and down the serpentine coast, past twisted pines and rocky coves where sea lions barked and surfed in the gigantic Pacific rollers. She was used to the Mediterranean's placidness; the Pacific Ocean was violent. Russia – where her mother was dying in the siege of Leningrad – lay on the other side, submerged in war, and it was as if the ferocity of battle, the storm of bombs and artillery barrages, the very destruction, flowed across in the huge waves. The Cadillac was her one deliverance. Cruising along, Gala was so small as to be invisible, a doll propped in the front seat. Yet she was an expert driver and would often head out with Dalí on Route 66, following it eastward all the way to New York and back. She did not dare meander from Route 66 for fear of getting lost.

In New York, Gala had much work. Along with his commissioned portraits, Dalí had also taken on the design for a ballet, *Colloque sentimentale*, inspired by Paul Verlaine's poem of the same name. Paul Bowles, the composer and writer, had been hired by the Marquis de Cuevas to compose the score. Bowles recounted to me his first meeting with Dalí and Gala, at a formal dinner given by an art gallery owner. Bowles, an intensely shy, and epicurean man, was seated next to Gala.

When the waiter brought out a bowl piled high with salad, Dalí began a long, droll story of how the 'Alp' of lettuce reminded him of a little girl who gets lost in the blizzard. The girl staggers until she can walk no more and then falls in the snow. A big St Bernard with a keg of cognac sniffs her out. Then Dalí says: 'The dog bends over the girl AND EATS HER UP!' It was very funny the way Dalí told it with his rolling Catalan accent.

Soon after, Gala leaned over to Bowles and said huskily: 'I want you to put me in a cage and feed me through the bars.'
'But why?' asked Bowles.
'Because it would give me pleasure.'
Bowles refused the invitation in the nicest possible way.

Music of any kind left Dalí lukewarm, and, as the Baron Philippe de Rothschild once found out, it could be difficult – and extremely costly – trying to persuade him to collaborate on ballets and operas. After many fruitless attempts at trying to entice Dalí into designing the décor for a ballet he was putting on, the baron finally approached Gala. Sauguet, the composer, who witnessed the meeting, told me that Gala replied: 'Fine, I'll get Dalí to do it, but I want payment. I want a diadem of diamonds.'

Desperate, Rothschild gave Gala her crown, and not long afterwards Dalí began supplying the baron with some rough ideas for décor. Baron Rothschild was dismayed, however. Dalí had envisaged some dancers on rollerskates, others hurtling down from the ceiling on suspension wires and a giant fire-extinguisher that would occasionally drench the audience. Whether or not he intended it, Dalí's ideas would never work, and the baron abandoned hope of any help from Dalí. All he had to show for his crown of diamonds was a few hasty sketches.

Gala's resentment towards aristocracy emerges in a similar anecdote told by the Prince de Faucigny-Lucinge, who had been one of Dalí's most loyal and helpful friends in the 1930s, having responded to Gala's pleas to save the starving Dalí from 'commercialising' himself by organising the Zodiac circle of patrons. For the prince it was a business deal and a way of helping an artist friend; but, for Gala, having to beg from the prince was a humiliation she never allowed herself to forget. The Prince de Faucigny-Lucinge also embodied the French society which Gala felt had always ridiculed her and merely tolerated her as shadow and keeper of the amusing Dalí. When she encountered him on a foray to New York, her resentment against the prince flared up. Dalí was famous and Gala felt no need to kowtow to the rich aristocrat. The prince told me: 'We hadn't met since before the war, and I said, "Gala how happy I am to see you." "You may be," she shrugged. "But me, not at all." ' With that insult, Gala wheeled away, leaving the prince stupefied.

From the mid–1940s onwards Gala seems to have become convinced that everyone – even her family – was grasping for a piece of Dalí's hard-earned fortune, and that she had to fight them off. Luis Buñuel was one unfortunate victim. Having surfaced in New York, penniless, with his wife and new baby, the film maker swallowed his pride and wrote to the Dalís asking for a loan of $50. Buñuel's son, Juan Luis, believes it was Gala who forced Dalí to turn his old school friend down. It is not surprising that Gala was ungenerous towards Buñuel; after all, he had tried strangling her once in Cadaqués.

Gala's lack of charity for her daughter, however, is less understandable. Even before Gala suspected that Cécile had secretly sold off the Dalí paintings left behind in the Paris apartment, there had been a distancing between mother and daughter. Cécile had divorced her first husband soon after his release from the German prisoner-of-war camp and in 1946 married a painter, Gérard Vulliamy. When Cécile announced she was pregnant, Gala – who had found it difficult enough to accept her own motherhood – was utterly repelled by the notion of becoming a grandmother. From New York, Gala posted packages of baby clothes for Cécile – all blue, for Gala vehemently hoped it would be a boy. Whatever spark of familial enthusiasm Gala may have shown was quickly snuffed out. In April 1947 Cécile gave birth to a girl. Gala's dislike of other females apparently began at the cradle.

Death and old age were two topics of conversation that Gala never discussed, and the birth of a granddaughter was a milestone that she preferred to ignore. 'Gala never stopped believing she was eighteen,' observed Reynolds Morse, a friend and collector of Dalí's work.

Once Gala found out that Cécile and her 'inferior' husband

had removed paintings from the Dalís' Paris flat, her rage was intense. Gala erroneously imagined that the paintings had been sold and wrote to her sister Lidia, fuming that many such paintings were ones that Dalí had wanted to donate to museums. 'Cécile is mean and petty bourgeois like her French grandmother,' Gala told her sister. The Victory Gift care packages from New York stopped arriving. Gala seems to have ceased supplying Eluard too. Perhaps she suspected Eluard's connivance in the disappearance of the paintings. Eluard, once again, implored Gala to be gentle with her daughter, who was recovering with difficulty from the recent birth. Cécile, who maintained that the paintings, far from being sold, had all been returned, was reduced to tears every time her mother's name was mentioned.

Eluard was himself in great suffering. Nusch, his frail replacement for Gala, had died of sudden brain haemorrhage in November 1946. Eluard may have carried a torch for Gala long after she left him, but Nusch's death left him in despair. The feud between Gala and Cécile can only have increased his depression. In addition, his lung problems grew progressively worse, and his hands trembled so severely that he could scarcely hold a pen.

Even Gala's relations with her sister Lidia were affected by her vindictiveness. Life in post-war Vienna was grim for Lidia and her family. Gala often sent packages and money orders – but in insignificant amounts. Once, in New York, she summoned Michael Stout, her lawyer, handed him a sealed envelope and told him to deliver it urgently to her sister in Vienna. Stout did so, and watched with curiosity as Lidia eagerly opened the letter. Inside was just a thousand dollars. Stout was stunned. His hourly legal fees, the return flight to Vienna and his expenses far exceeded Gala's gift to Lidia. When he asked Gala why she had gone to the trouble for such a small sum, she snapped back: 'Because that's all my sister deserves.'

The people who were probably Gala and Dalí's closest friends through the years were Reynolds Morse and his wife Eleanor. A more unlikely collector of Dalí's unhinged fantasies is hard to imagine. Morse is a plain-talking Coloradan who wears cowboy hats and string ties clasped with a moss agate. He is also rich – his family owned mines in Colorado. Reynolds Morse himself was fascinated by machines; in his twenties he invented a moulding press that revolutionised the plastics industry. Aside from designing machines and climbing mountains, Morse was obsessed with western art and the science fiction of an obscure Caribbean Creole writer named M. P. Shiel, who was a contemporary of Robert Louis Stevenson.

In 1942 he and Eleanor wandered into the Manhattan gallery of George Keller and saw a small canvas entitled *Daddy Longlegs of the Evening-Hope*. It was certainly nothing like Morse's cowboy paintings of the Rockies, but the canvas intrigued him. 'All the other artists were painting baskets with flowers. This challenged you to find out what it all meant.' The gallery owner told Morse that Dalí and his wife were staying at the St Regis Hotel, so Morse wrote Dalí a note requesting to see him. They met in the hotel's King Cole Bar and, despite Dalí's garbled English, became friends. Over the years Morse was to see many ugly faces of Dalí – his cruelty and cowardice, his greed and extreme perversity – but his conviction of Dalí's genius never wavered.

Gala, however, shocked Morse. As he explained to me:

> She invited me up to their room. Dalí wasn't around. Gala brought out some of Dalí's erotic drawings and then said something like: 'There's more where that came from.' And then she propositioned me.
>
> I said 'No' as politely as I could. Gala wasn't my type. Besides, I'd just gotten married to Eleanor and Gala was old enough to be my mother. Thank God she wasn't, though.
>
> Even after all the years, I don't think that Gala ever really forgave me.

Another unwilling quarry was Jimmy, the teenage son of Max Ernst. Once Jimmy encountered Gala in New York. After telling him, 'I knew you as a small baby,' Gala began playing footsie with him while they shared blinis in the Russian Tea Room. Gala had broken up Max Ernst's marriage in Cologne with Jimmy's Jewish mother, and the youngster was aghast that this woman, who had so influenced the course of his own life, now wanted to seduce him. Gala reminded Jimmy of 'an unchaste Diana of the Hunt after the kill . . . in constant wait for unnamed sensualities'. He was afraid, having for so long heard his mother revile Gala as a 'slinking, glittering creature'. When Gala invited him up to her hotel room, Jimmy left the restaurant without saying a word. Gala was furious. Several days later, Jimmy had the misfortune to run into her and Dalí. 'You're a shit! A monster!' she spat out.

When Jimmy Ernst again encountered Gala, twenty-four years later, she had still not forgotten the episode nor forgiven him. 'I am very angry with you. You behaved very badly that day. We could have had such a pleasant afternoon.'

Dalí's reaction was curious. 'You were not nice at all. I remember it well,' Dalí told Jimmy. 'I was ill that day . . . I wouldn't have disturbed you.'

While Jimmy avoided Gala after her failed seduction, the Morses never let her behaviour interfere with their appreciation of Dalí. Despite Gala's icy vindictiveness, the Morses were to become Dalí's most stalwart collectors and supporters. He and Eleanor bought more of Dalí's works than anyone else; their museum in St Petersburg, Florida, contains 93 oil paintings, 200 watercolours and over 1000 graphics and sculptures. They also travelled around the USA by train with the Dalís in the 1950s, translating the artist's lectures. 'It was great fun, but there came a time when Eleanor and I had to get back to the business and the kids. So we slipped a goodbye note under their compartment door and left the train. Next time we saw them, Gala was still angry. "How could you abandon Dalí?" she shrieked.'

Only once did Gala ask Morse for advice – on investment. 'Gala asked me what I thought of New York City Bonds. I said, "Don't do it." Did she listen? No, Gala went out and spent £750,000 on the city bonds, and she ended up losing a lot of money,' recalled Morse. 'She was like that, stubborn.'

Gala had flashes of kindness, though; when Eleanor Morse was once bedridden, Gala brought her flowers and a jumper. The Morses made it their business to help the Dalís and Morse was to become a tireless defender of Dalí's art: when Dalí and Gala were being manipulated by unscrupulous dealers and assistants, Morse fought to clear Dalí's name; when Gala and Dalí both grew old and sick, Morse cared for them and found them hospitals and good doctors. The Morses found Gala and Dalí to be companions who were charming but who ultimately never dropped their guard for over four decades. Reynolds Morse commented: 'We tried to be friends but they always treated us as clients, as pigeons to be plucked.'

13

A Floating Madonna

It was high summer, August 1948, and Dalí had no doubt that his father and sister would be at their family home on the Cadaqués beach, escaping from the scorching Ampurdan plain. Dalí was nervous. He and his father had patched up their grievances – partially – before Dalí went to America; but this time Dalí had Gala with him – the whore, the Russian drug trafficker. Dalí's father had gone so far as to try to prevent his son's civil marriage in France by blackening Gala's name.

Gala and Dalí decided that the old man might be enraged by seeing her. While Dalí knocked on the door of his father's house at Cadaqués, Gala hung back, hidden from view. The father, a huge-bellied man, gave Dalí a bear hug and seemed overjoyed to see his son. Nervously Dalí pressed a gift-wrapped present into his father's arms. It was a velvet dressing-gown, bought from one of the best New York department stores, one that accentuated the father's Jovian aura, or so Dalí believed. The cries of excitement from Dalí's father had attracted the others from inside the house – first Dalí's stepmother (his former aunt) and then, warily, his sister, Ana Maria.

Dalí explained how they had sailed from New York to Le Havre, and from Paris travelled by express train to Port Bou – with 950 kilos of luggage. Their belongings were humped on to two hired cars, and the trip over the coastal mountains was on the scale of Hannibal's. Those were just the bare necessities. There was more on the way by freighter, arriving in a week, dozens of crates and a gleaming black Cadillac, the likes of which had never been seen before in Spain. Even the US ambassador to the dictator's court in Madrid did not have a Cadillac as new as Dalí's.

Gala would drive this millionaire's sedan. And where was

Gala, asked Dalí's family. Sheepishly, Dalí turned and called down the cobble-stoned street. Gala emerged from behind some fishing boats that had been dragged up on to the rocky beach. She wore a black bow in her hair and looked tiny and forlorn, like a schoolgirl caught out in a game of hide and seek. Ana Maria reportedly spat on the floor as Gala approached the doorway.

Dalí gave Ana Maria a present that would end up being a time bomb for him. It was a copy of his autobiography, *The Secret Life of Salvador Dalí*. Dalí's venomous depictions of his childhood infuriated his sister so much that she set the record straight with a book of her own. *Salvador Dalí Seen by his Sister* was a modest book, but it pricked holes in Dalí's own attempts to inflate the angst of his childhood to an epic scale. Young Dalí emerges as a gifted but awfully spoiled brat in an ordinary middle-class household. When Ana Maria's book was published in 1949, Dalí howled at the double-cross and vowed never to forgive her.

The Port Lligat house was a mess. Its walls bore the graffiti of passing anarchists and their fascist pursuers. Its floors were scorched by cooking fires. Lidia, La Bien Plantada (the Well-planted One), a holy fool of a woman who had been their cook and caretaker, had died that year. The house was uninhabitable. Dalí's father would not hear of them staying in a hotel while cleaners scoured out the traces of war from the Port Lligat home. The couple stayed, for the first time, with Dalí's family. Several days after Dalí and Gala's arrival in Cadaqués, a Catalan journalist came to the house at the artist's request. Dalí's father listened, with a good deal of amazement, as his rebellious and athestic son, whom he had raised as a good liberal, explained his ideas of a religious renaissance in art and embraced the Franco dictatorship. This seemingly genuine conversion served a purpose: it brought Dalí under the protection of the authoritarian state. Isolated by most of Europe, Generalissimo Franco was desperate for credibility. If American students arrived in Spain for a two-week tour, their movements were covered by the right-wing daily, *ABC*, with a wealth of detail formerly reserved for visiting heads of state. Of all Spain's renowned artists, Dalí was the only one to return home.

Gala's charms – and the wealth she had obviously helped Dalí amass – eventually won over the father. Under Franco's law, no marriages performed before the dictatorship or outside Spain were recognised, and that included Dalí and Gala's 1934 marriage in France. Therefore, if Gala were to abandon Dalí or if Dalí were to die, his family would inherit. (Gala eventually realised this danger: at her insistence, she and Dalí were remarried in a religious ceremony on 8 August 1958 at a small chapel outside Gerona.)

Slowly, though, the father thawed to Gala. He also loved riding with her in the black Cadillac, showing off in front of his cronies at the cafés and social clubs along Figueras's main boulevard. Her feet hardly reached the pedals, but Gala was a skilful driver. One friend, Isidoro Bea, said that if any motorist dared to obstruct them Gala would speed up and curse the offender in her best Catalan. Franco had outlawed the Catalan language, its flag and even the local dances on the grounds that they were treasonous, but Gala was invulnerable as the wife of Generalissimo Franco's most honoured painter. Once the military commander of Catalonia remarked archly that Gala spoke the regional language of Catalan better than she did Spanish. 'It's almost as strange as you not bothering to learn Catalan,' she told the general. Gala and Dalí often took his father on cruises to Cape Creus, where they picnicked, relived childhood memories and together watched the rocky coastline strangely transform with the passing clouds, revealing hidden angels, eagles and titanic heads. The old man was crippled, and these excursions by boat and Cadillac cheered him immeasurably. One relative observed: 'Dalí's father was always friendly to Gala. It took them a while, but eventually they got on well.'

Ana Maria was less yielding; her jealousy of Gala never diminished. Gala had been treated coldly by Eluard's mother-in-law in the early days of her marriage to the poet, but Ana Maria showed pure and unconcealed hatred. She hated Gala for 'stealing' her brother's devotion; she hated Gala, unjustly, because she suspected her of having informed on her to the torturers of the military police; and she hated Gala for giving the world the impression that all Dalí wanted was money.

By the late 1940s Dalí's artistic reputation was sliding. If the money was good he would lend his name to any product, no matter how trivial. He did portraits of rich men's wives and one of a Hollywood studio boss with his dachshund, a canvas which hung in the dog's kennel. The very fetishes that Dalí had dreamed up – his soft watches, crutches and jelly shapes – had grown stale, devoid of shock value; they had become his commercial trademark, and he had retailed them too often. In conversation Dalí had a tendency to repeat himself, telling the same silly jokes of his Ampurdan childhood again and again. His two autobiographies, *The Secret Life* and *The Unspeakable Confessions of Salvador Dalí*, tread the same territory twice. His paintings had become equally predictable. In addition, surrealism had gone as limp as a Dalí timepiece. Abstract art was what the galleries were clamouring for now.

And, of course, there was the bomb. For Dalí, his paranoiac-critical method and the theories of the subconscious he had ransacked from Freud were melted away by Hiroshima's heat. Dalí was searching for unity, for something outside the banal mechanics of mind, something that could bear witness to the universe that lay beyond the shattered atom. That something was religion. Dalí believed that only in Spain, in the land of such mystics as St Teresa of Avila and St John of the Cross, could he find inspiration. Gala, however, had been in no hurry to leave the United States. She was giving up the many luxuries of New York and California, the music, the films and her young male companions.

Slowly Dalí's mysticism took form, and the shape it assumed was Gala. He painted her as the Madonna of Port Lligat, in angelic levitation above the fishermen in their boats on the sea. There was no change in Gala's behaviour to warrant this idealisation – she was still the prowling seductress of young men, the arrogant and ruthless keeper of Dalí. It was not as though Gala necessarily inspired his epiphany. Nanita Kalachnikov, a Spanish beauty who was married to a Russian aristocrat and was Dalí's companion from the 1950s onwards, told me: 'Gala was religious but not in the ordinary sense. She prayed a lot but always alone. She wasn't that clear on faith. My husband, who was Russian Orthodox, got very frustrated with Gala because she seemed to know so very little about the Russian church.' Gala was also plagued by her sense of having sinned. A Sunday ritual developed in the Dalí home; as the maid prepared herself for the walk over the hill to Cadaqués for mass, Gala would call down to her: 'Pray for me. You're a better person that I am, and God will pay more attention to you.' None of the servants was under the impression that Gala was jesting.

However, Dalí's biographer, Meryle Secrest, suggests that Gala's canonisation reflected a change in Dalí's psyche. 'Just as she . . . was from now on to be put on a pedestal as the Virgin Mary, so he, who had spent so many years trying to come to terms with male–female sexuality, had settled into his role of voyeur and given up.' There is in Dalí a bit of the hair-shirted ascetic. On the surface Dalí did not mind Gala's infidelities. Nanita Kalachnikov was once with Dalí when Gala answered a telephone call from her current lover. 'Isn't that so-o-o nice?' cooed Dalí. 'See, he loves her and that makes Gala very, very happy.' The closest Dalí had ever come to referring directly to Gala's adultery occurred in a conversation with Oriol Maspons, a Catalan photographer. Maspons recalled:

Dalí was posing for me out on the terrace in his cowboy shirt and with one of his many canes. This one's handle was curved up slightly like horns. Jokingly, I told Dalí not to put it too close to his head because it would look like the horns of a cuckold. At that moment, Gala went sailing out of Port Lligat with her young man and a great big bottle of Anis del Mono. Dalí pointed and said: 'Moi je suis le roi des cocus.' ['I'm the king of cuckolds.']

Dalí's inability to satisfy Gala – if any permanent partner could – must have tormented him, though, and there could be truth in what Secrest says. Dalí often boasted about what Gala did for him sexually, with more lyricism than conviction. His orgasms were architectonic visions – basilicas, domes and spirals – but not once did Dalí ever explain what he did for Gala. The silence is suspect. Dalí's sexual arousal had always been dependent on his voyeuristic fantasies, and although Dalí insisted that Gala was the only creature with whom he could reach orgasm, he seems to have abandoned any attempt at ordinary marital sex in order to indulge in more bizarre visual pleasures. Whether or not this occurred out of frustration or because Gala ceased to stir his eroticism, it was easier to elevate Gala to a spiritual mother than to accept her as a wife, an equal.

Although Dalí's role with her had transformed, he still signed her name with his on the bottom right corner of his canvases – a privilege she earned. In 1956 she encouraged him to hire an assistant, and he chose Isidoro Bea, a commercial artist whose resemblance to Pablo Picasso was a source of mischievous delight for Dalí. Whenever he was plagued with doubt about being less talented than Picasso, Dalí would abuse Bea. His task was to divide Dalí's canvases into geometric sections to plot the perspective and then paint in the inevitable background of cloud wisps, sea and Port Lligat coastline. 'Gala thought that I would help Dalí discipline himself,' said Bea. 'He was terribly anarchic. Sometimes he wouldn't paint for fifteen days and then he'd throw himself into it furiously. Dalí would say: "Isn't this stupendous?" and I'd reply gruffly: "We'll see when it's finished." '

Bea was surprised that, although she herself never painted, Gala was an efficient helper capable of stretching the canvases on their frame, then applying the 'underpaint' using formulae which she had written down in a notebook along with colour mixtures. 'Gala never picked up a brush herself,' Bea told me, 'but she was a good judge. When Dalí finished a painting, Gala would sit down and give a lengthy critique. "This eye droops too much," she would say. "There's more intensity on this side of the canvas than the other." Many times she would be right and Dalí, grumbling, would make the corrections.'

Dalí, like any great artist, knew when he had reached a dead end. When one style had been exhausted, a crisis would slowly envelop him. Alone, he lacked the courage to evolve. It was Gala's determination that helped drag Dalí over his artistic barriers. She helped him shed the skin of his old technique, as he moved from Freudian dream depictions to religious classicism and on to the geometric tricks of op art.

In 1948, when they returned to Spain, Gala was fifty-three and looked her age. The black bow that Coco Chanel prescribed for her hair, and which Gala wore piously, made her look like Minnie Mouse with no tail. Dalí was ten years younger and still darkly handsome. Wherever the couple went, mingling with millionaires and dukes, film actors and government ministers, it was always Dalí who was the centre of attention, Dalí *le divin*. This irritated Gala, who felt she was not getting due credit for Dalí's success. Dalí may have raved about Gala, worshipped her volubly, but to outsiders her aura was imperceptible through her arrogance and bad temper. 'The French in high society can be terrible snobs,' Nanita Kalachnikov told me. 'They loved Dalí. He was charming, so flamboyant. But they treated Gala very badly. What did they care that she had been married to Eluard, or been the mistress of Max Ernst? She was no longer pretty. To them she was a mean, little middle-class woman. And this hurt Gala very much.' At Dalí's coaxing, Gala would don her evening gown, usually one of Chanel's ten-year-old hand-me-downs, and appear briefly at grand balls with Dalí; but Gala would only stay long enough for Dalí to overcome his inital jitters at the party, then she would slip into a taxi for a rendezvous with one of her young men.

These brief command performances were enough to persuade her old friends that Gala had changed, for the worse. Max Ernst, whose relations with Dalí had ended sourly in the 1920s, remarked that Gala had become 'a parody of a woman'. Léonor Fini, more charitably, found her distant: 'She had become a personage and she wore this like an armour, very closed up inside herself.' Gala was even harsher with the many women who flitted around Dalí. Nanita Kalachnikov observed: 'Gala was consumed by jealousy. She thought that another woman, younger and prettier, would steal Dalí away from her – after all the hard times she had dragged him through. She was very suspicious of other women – of me. It wasn't until two years before her death that she finally realised I wasn't trying to take Dalí away from her. She kept ringing me up from her Pubol castle, full of remorse. Once she tried joking: "What a shame we're not lesbians." '

However, Gala was not given to grief. In 1952 Eluard died, having succeeded in living up to his own modest goal of 'not dishonouring poetry'. Eluard had always opposed cheap patriotism, but he was buried as a national hero. Schoolchildren across France had memorised his poem, 'Liberty', which during the German occupation RAF planes had parachuted down in bundles to raise courage among the resistance fighters. His funeral ceremony was attended by Jean Cocteau, Picasso, Louis Aragon, Elsa Triolet and hundreds of other admirers. Condolence messages arrived from Pablo Neruda in Chile, Bertolt Brecht in Berlin. Eluard's third wife, Dominique, a dark-haired beauty whom Eluard had met during a peace conference in Mexico, was there. Gala was not.

After Eluard's burial, Gala approached Cécile. It was the first time that Gala had deigned speak to Cécile for four years, but if Cécile had expected Eluard's death to bring any forgiveness from her mother she was wrong. Gala told her daughter that she never wanted to see her again.

This was the woman whom Dalí was painting as the loving Virgin Mother. In the *Madonna of Port Lligat* Gala's smile is so beatific as to be utterly false. There is no soaring spirituality here – or even human love. The Gala Madonna looks curiously brittle, as though she were a hollow plaster figurine about to shatter into a thousand shards and shower into the sea once Dalí's levitation trick finishes. The same classical stillness pervades Dalí's other religious and mythological portraits of Gala. It is as if Dalí, by draining the sex from his object of veneration, has rendered Gala so chaste as to be inhuman and unconvincing.

It took Dalí a good three years after falling in love with Gala to feature her prominently on canvas. In his earlier work Gala staged small guest appearances, swept into a corner with Dalí's strange debris. Aside from two classical portraits, it was not until 1933 with *Gala and the Angelus of Millet Preceding the Imminent Arrival of the Conic Anamorphoses* that Gala was awarded more than a walk-on part. Here she is disturbing and certainly not attractive. Gala grins rather demonically from beneath an over-sized seaman's cap. The effect is unsettling. Then, in 1935, *Portrait of Gala* showed her looking as dumpy and severe as the peasant woman in the painting of Millet's *Angelus* which hangs above her. In his erotic writings Dalí would have us believe that he found Gala to be a sexual, desirable woman – as did Eluard and a great many other surrealists – but Dalí could not paint this aspect of her nature, at least not by showing her face. His most erotic portrait of Gala is a nude study of her back. She sits with her legs crossed as if she were waiting on a rumpled bed for another session with her lover. There is only a hint of her strong, Slavic cheekbones in profile.

In one of the more remarkable portraits of Gala, executed in 1975, her shirt is opened, revealing one breast. (One is reminded of the 'gift' Eluard was given in being allowed to slip a hand inside her blouse.) Her arms are crossed, not in modesty but in defiance; her lips are closed and firm. She has all the self-convic-tion of a Joan of Arc, but none of her religious humanity. Gala's determined sensuality is all the more sinister because she is wearing a bracelet of an emerald dragon with ruby eyes. She looks dangerous, as indeed she must have seemed to Dalí with his raging sexual insecurity.

However, the irony of portraying celestial Galas was not intended. Without Gala's guard-dog meanness Dalí knew he would have been besieged by unscrupulous con-men. He also knew that only under Gala's protection could his art flourish. Dalí was superstitious, and Gala was a kind of magic charm, one he could not forsake even if at times she terrified him.

Dalí's mystical embrace did not make him chaste; if anything, it brought about an explosion of his sexual fantasies. 'Eroticism,' he wrote, 'is the royal road to the soul of God.' Dalí was swift to realise that one of the perks of being a famous artist of legendary extravagance was that he never lacked young and beautiful people willing to 'model' whatever scene the artist dreamed. Invariably, Dalí's fantasies centred on sodomy. In a chapter entitled 'How to Pray to God Without Believing in Him' in his second 'autobiography', Dalí recounts with relish how he orchestrated the buggery of a Spanish girl by her lover for the benefit of himself and another spectator. He describes the 'angelic vision' of the girl, arching backwards to kiss her lover as he sodomised her. Says Dalí: 'I have never been able to tell this story without each time having the wonderful feeling that I had violated the secret of perfect beauty.' Often he revelled in hovering over the performing couple, directing the rhythm of a caress, the fall of the girl's long hair on her partner's body, even measuring the extent of anal penetration with his cane. It made a better spectacle, said Dalí, if the couple happened to be in love. Just as often, as the couple's rising rhythms made them oblivious to anything but their own pleasure, Dalí would order them to stop and then cast out the humiliated pair. Then Dalí would fall to his knees, laughing hysterically.

I am in an unaccustomed dimension, an absolute where only the *quality of God* reigns: a totally irrational universe in which everything is sublime and transcended, and my joy itself is a mystical delirium. There is no longer any vice or virtue, good or evil, flesh or spirit – orgasm becomes ecstasy and fulfilment of mind. I attain a harmony that is located in the very space of the soul.

Then Dalí would pick up his brushes and begin work at his easel.

For all his stratospheric talk of soul, Dalí's behaviour smacks of little more than a pathetic attempt to inflict his sexual inadequacy on his bewildered hirelings. Perhaps for this reason Dalí's erotic rituals were not to Gala's taste. She refused the role of either spectator or participant. Gala needed privacy and concentration to weave a sexual spell around her victims. When Dalí writes that these voyeuristic orgies caused her suffering, it is with glee. One senses a glimmer of the same hysterical streak of cruelty that Dalí showed when Gala was ill with pleurisy and he almost killed her with his smothering embraces – a revenge, possibly, for her sexual appetite. A woman friend of Dalí's, who disliked Gala and preferred not to be identified, said: 'Dalí simply didn't want Gala there. Dalí liked watching – and masturbating. Gala would have wanted to be at the heart of this bacchanalia, and this, of course, would have wrecked it for Dalí.'

In November 1949, nearly a year after Dalí returned to Spain and launched his crusade for a religious revival in art, he had finished the *Madonna of Port Lligat* and wanted it blessed by the Pope. This was a gamble: the Vatican's head of protocol was likely to glance through Dalí's press cuttings and slam the doors on him. But Dalí managed to arrange a private interview with Pope Pius XII. The pontiff was reportedly impressed by the *Madonna of Port Lligat* and perhaps a bit bemused by the extravagant claims that this surrealist, with his moustache twisted into horns stiffened by date-sugar, would be the twentieth century's unlikely saviour of Christian art.

Port Lligat was not New York or Paris; the number of beautiful subjects that Dalí and Gala could lure into their separate webs was much reduced. The commerce of such arrangements was also unseemly. They needed a go-between, someone who could handle the logistics of finding – or hiring – young specimens for the Dalís' pleasure, as well as arranging their yearly migrations and the expanding sales of the artist's work. The burden was too much for Gala alone. They needed a fixer.

The fixer could also bring order to their chaotic finances. Gala was a compulsive hoarder; her purse would be bursting with cheques for several thousand dollars which she could never bring herself to deposit. The Dalís had a habit of employing people informally from one day to the next.

If Dalí wanted a rhinoceros horn or a diving suit or a model willing to coat herself in chocolate, the fixer would somehow provide. If Gala wanted the company of a young boy who spoke Russian, a blond or a Mediterranean type who looked like Dalí in his youth, then the fixer would make the necessary introductions.

If Dalí wanted a plastic phallus and a boy who would consent to be sodomised by the apparatus, the fixer would arrange it. If Dalí needed a girl who would place a lighted straw in her vagina so that he could observe – from the sanitary distance of three metres – her expression as the flame singed her pubic hair, then the fixer would provide. One guest at Port Lligat recalled that one of Dalí's male groupies eagerly offered to perform the 'sewing machine' – the artist's coy name for the sexual act – with his girlfriend for an after-lunch entertainment. Dalí of course agreed, and afterwards commented: 'X makes a good sewing machine, don't you think?'

During the permissiveness of the 1960s, Dalí's 'erotic masses' ceased being discreet affairs and he was able to broaden the canvas of his fantasies. He hired palaces and populated them with dwarfs and transvestites, trapeze artists and ocelots. A friend invited to one soirée recalled: 'Dalí loved giving tours around his parties. Every bedroom would have different couples – men and women, men and men, women and women – you name it. Some important people were there too, French state ministers. And it was all for Dalí's delectation.'

Gala wants were more simple but abundant. 'She was a true nymphomaniac,' said a woman friend of Dalí's, who wished to remain anonymous. She added:

I think it was the classic case of a woman who was never satisfied sexually and she had to keep trying with every man she crossed. Once she broke down and said that she hated doctors because once, in Paris, a doctor had 'emptied' her 'completely'.

Gala could be so belligerent about sex. Once we were having lunch in Duran's with Generalissimo Franco's granddaughter, Carmen, and her husband, Alfonso de Borbon-Dampierre. Alfonso's brother, Gonzalo, was with us too. Immediately, Gala started putting her hands all over Alfonso. The poor man was in such a state. He was never very bright, but Alfonso at least was sweet.

First there was a scene because the waiter spilled a bucket of ice all over my hair, and Gala demanded that he be sacked. I didn't care, but I could see why Gala would if it had happened to her. Gala's hair was so thin. She had to work at her hair a lot. She was very protective towards me then. The only time ever, really.

Then, as Gala and Dalí were leaving, there began an embarrassing comedy of errors. Almost like Mae West, Gala said to Alfonso: 'Come see me some time in Paris. We're at the Meurice.'

'Delighted,' replied Alfonso.

'What do you mean?' snapped Gala. 'How can you say yes when you don't even know where the Meurice is?'

'But I do,' Alfonso protested amiably. 'I used to visit my grandfather there.'

'It's on rue Rivoli,' Gala persisted. 'Wait a minute. Your grandfather, why, did he work there in the hotel?' she added, confusing Alfonso with one of her rented boyfriends.

'No,' replied Alfonso. 'My grandfather was a guest. He was the King of Spain, Alfonso XIII.'

14

Autumn Cannibalism

On a street in Brooklyn, Gala suddenly ordered the driver of her Cadillac to stop. In that part of Brooklyn a Cadillac was a novelty, a provocation, and the winos and drug addicts, roused from their conspiracies of stupor, lurched out towards the car. The situation had become dangerous. The driver's impulse was to speed away before the derelicts pushed past the rubbish bins and closed in on the Cadillac, but Gala was oblivious to the growing threat. She had lowered her window and was calling out in her rough English.

She had seen a figure in a tenement doorway, a young man, thin as a needle. He was handsome; she beckoned him over. The resemblance was remarkable. His dark Mediterranean looks reminded her of Salvador Dalí as a young man – except that the intensity of this boy's eyes was fired by heroin. He was called William Rotlein, and he lived on drugs, tins of dog food and goods stolen from supermarkets.

Gala invited him into the Cadillac, and this was the start of their love affair. It was 1963; she was sixty-seven and Rotlein in his early twenties.

The Dalís were making one of their by now frequent visits to New York and staying at the St Regis Hotel. The St Regis concierge was accustomed to the Dalís' strange guests, but this newcomer – for whom Gala commandeered a room next to hers – exuded menace. She ushered the derelict up to one of New York's most expensive hotel rooms and bathed him. It was apparent that Rotlein was an addict; his arms were pitted with needle holes redder than ants. Gala's own direct experience with drug addiction was probably limited; the surrealists may have dabbled in opium or hashish but only dared do so behind André Breton's back. Dalí too had no need of strong drugs to induce his hallucinations or escape from them. Yet she had the sense to realise that she could not cut Rotlein off heroin without giving him a substitute – alcohol. For days she kept Rotlein captive inside his hotel suite, giving him all the food, whisky and champagne he wanted. There was still no sex; Gala busied herself as his nurse.

Gala's cure succeeded. Occasionally Rotlein would take money from her purse and escape, but either he would wander back or Gala would track him down in Central Park. One way or another he always returned, and soon his dependence on Gala was almost as great as it had been on heroin. This was probably how Gala had planned it. Rotlein's helplessness had touched her as had Dalí's beauty, vulnerability and madness a long time ago.

She was also rebelling against the role of Mrs Dalí. In a rare interview, Gala said that she wanted to 'live her life as a constant explosion'. Increasingly, this was becoming an explosion of rage. From the 1960s onwards, Gala was less willing to play the public role of high priestess at the Dalí oracle. She dismissed most of Dalí's retinue of admirers and hangers-on as 'monsters' and shunned their company. It was not a complete abdication; she simply chose to exercise her power capriciously and with growing malevolence.

Gala grew more sadistic, hostile and intolerant. If someone annoyed her, she was likely to spit in his face or, worse, grab a lighted cigarette and stub it out on his bare skin. Anyone ugly or deformed would be dismissed from her presence. In a way, Gala's attitude was understandable. The greediest kinds of art dealer, publisher and con-artist would swarm around Dalí like the flies that the artist encouraged to land on his long, sticky moustache.

Rotlein became another cause for Gala. She threw herself into his resurrection with all the fanaticism she had previously reserved for Dalí alone. He could not paint, write or even speak coherently. He stole and was drunk most of the time. Yet Gala was convinced that Rotlein had the talent to become a great film actor. She dragged him off to Rome, Florence, Turin and Verona. The couple swore eternal love at Romeo and Juliet's tomb, and then they began having sex. Often they stayed at the Turin mansion of the Albarettos, who were wealthy collectors of Dalí. 'There was no doubt that the two of them were making love. They'd rise from bed at two in the afternoon and still be laughing and embracing each other at the breakfast table.' Gala confided to Mrs Mara Albaretto that she loved Rotlein as much as she had loved anyone since Eluard. 'And that included Dalí,' said Mrs Albaretto.

The Italian popular press soon fastened on to this strange love affair between the Grandmother and the Boy, as the mismatched couple were described. A few of the romance magazines claimed that Gala intended to divorce Dalí and marry Rotlein. This was a rumour that Rotlein, motivated in equal proportions by love and opportunism, actively encouraged. Once, in Rome, Gala and Rotlein were photographed fighting in the street because she had refused to pose with him. Not only did she want to avoid the scandal reaching Dalí in Spain, but she also feared that the glare of the flashbulbs would be enough to break her spell. Although she might convince herself that she had a twenty-year-old's energy and that she could bedazzle a young lover, the camera was harder to fool.

The Albarettos were worried that Gala's scandalous behaviour would end up staining Dalí's reputation. 'What can I do?' Dalí had asked them over the telephone from Port Lligat. 'My Olivette is in love.' (Olivette was one of his many nicknames for Gala.) In the beginning, Dalí welcomed her infatuation with his younger lookalike. He called him Adil, an inversion of his own name, and often sketched him at Gala's insistence.

In Rome, Gala pulled strings to arrange for Federico Fellini to give Rotlein a screen test. Afterwards, the film director laughed and said frankly: 'This boy has the face of a bandit, and Italy is filled with men who look like bandits.'

After Gala's romance had dragged on for several weeks, Rotlein's insistence that she divorce Dalí began to annoy and confuse her. Using the excuse that Dalí had summoned her back temporarily, Gala left Rotlein in Turin with the Albarettos. 'I think he really loved her. He had ripped two buttons off Gala's coat and he was always moping over them,' recalled Mrs Albaretto. Gala's absence eroded Rotlein's tottering hold on sanity. He threatened suicide, and stood naked on the high window-ledge of the Albarettos' mansion. Neighbours complained and the police wanted to arrest him.

The Albarettos appealed to Gala, who arranged for Rotlein to fly back first class to New York. 'Dalí had received some medal from the Spanish government and Gala seemed to think that, with all the bad press, her affair with Rotlein might be courting trouble,' said Mrs Albaretto. When Rotlein begged to be allowed to visit her in Port Lligat, Gala refused, yet she continued making telephone calls to him daily.

Gala found it hard to be faithful to anyone. Those who defend Gala – few in number – describe her as a nymphomaniac. Rotlein had taken their Romeo and Juliet vows more seriously than she; as soon as Gala began to feel trapped by his demands, she cut him off. Then, in rapid succession, she took on a string of semi-permanent lovers, starting with a Greek pianist whom she called Analysis. Then she seduced a dark-haired philosopher named Michel Pastore. 'It wasn't just the money that attracted him to Gala,' said Enrique Sabater, Dalí's new private secretary. 'When she dropped Michel he was truly broken up. I don't know what it was about her.' After his experience with Gala, Michel retreated to a monastery near Avignon.

Another lover allegedly robbed Gala of her jewellery and several Dalí works. In the mid–1970s, Gala's current companion volunteered to drive Gala up through southern France to catch a transatlantic liner at Le Havre. They stopped along the road at a restaurant. While he and Gala were eating, the young man's friends reportedly stole her suitcase from the car containing some jewellery designed by Chanel and several valuable Dalí paintings. A friend of Dalí's recalled: 'It was very hard for Gala to accept that this boy was with her for the money. Dalí was very gentle and forgiving that time.' Gala refused to press charges against the boy.

Gala's excursions with young men were a regular part of her life in the 1960s and 1970s. Amanda Lear, a companion of Dalí's claims in her memoirs that Gala's going rate for a gigolo was $10,000. However, Sabater dismissed this: 'Gala never paid for it. She didn't have to.' Sometimes these young men were agency models, out-of-work actors or mediocre painters. Her seduction line with these painters was usually unswerving: she would convince them that her passion would inspire them to true artistry. One witness to Gala's many seductions (who preferred not to be identified) was more cynical: 'They were making love to Gala but only because they wanted something from Dalí: money, paintings, a part of the action.'

Occasionally Gala descended from the Alfonso XIII suite in the Hotel Meurice or from their eyrie in the St Regis to attend Dalí's

Paupers' Tea – Dalí's name for the audience of philosophers, beautiful young actors and actresses, millionaires, transvestites and assorted oddballs who happened to amuse him. The actress Mia Farrow was a regular, as were Ultra Violet, Paul Morrisey and other avant-garde renegades from Andy Warhol's factory. Dalí would have the most handsome men parade in front of Gala, and those who passed approval would be selected as her seating companions. Their degree of responsiveness would determine Gala's next step. Reynolds Morse recalled: 'At these crazy dinners, Gala would be stroking some beautiful boy whose eyes would stray across the table to more fertile pastures – the breasts of a young model, someone of the boy's own age. Gala would notice this and stroke her boy more persistently. It must have hurt her, but that's the way she was.'

When the Dalís were in Paris, the doormen at the Hotel Meurice would often help Gala load her suitcases into the battered Citroën Deux Chevaux of her young companion. Gala would disappear for as long as two weeks with her lovers. If she was in Europe and the weather was warm, they would drive across France into the Swiss Alps, where as a teenager Gala had fallen in love with Eluard. For a woman who professed to ignore the past, Gala could be inescapably nostalgic; or perhaps these escapades were a way for her to stop the clock, conquer her ageing. It was rejuvenating for Gala, in her seventies, to be with a boy as fresh as Eluard had been at the Clavadel sanatorium.

In winter Gala would retreat with her boyfriend to a small flat which the Dalís had bought in Monte Carlo to establish residency in the Principality for tax reasons. This trysting place was discreet; the photographers who clustered around Dalí seldom chased after Gala. If anyone knew of Gala's affairs, they were hushed up, even in staunchly Catholic Spain, out of reverence for *el Maestro*.

Had Gala been a man, this lasciviousness would perhaps have been regarded with admiration instead of repugnance. When an old man cavorts with a teenage prostitute he is applauded for his sexual stamina, envied for his energy and good fortune, while the same act by an octogenarian female is considered unspeakably perverse. It is a testimony to both Gala's personal power and her cynicism that she was able to flout this convention. As for Dalí, he confessed to jealousy but said that Gala's infidelities spurred his creativity. On her return to Port Lligat he would ceremonially play a popular tune of the time, 'Baby Come Back'.

In a way, Gala relied on Dalí's artistry to keep her young, for despite her protests she was obviously pleased when Dalí insisted on painting her. Once in the late 1960s when Gala found out that Dalí had hired a shapely Dutch model, Mia Rentjens, to pose for some silhouettes, Gala offered her own services instead, on the pretext that she would be cheaper than the Dutch girl. Dalí complied, and the completed silhouettes were of Gala's taut profile. Dalí's depictions of Gala were always photographically accurate, but he often left out the wrinkles. Painting Gala's face never ceased to be a frightening challenge for Dalí. As he entered in his diary: 'It is because of the fear of touching Gala's face that I will finally be able to paint!' He added: 'I must take the whole of Gala's face courageously.'

Being sadistic with others did not stop Gala from being brutal with herself. She celebrated her seventieth birthday in 1967. From then on, any photograph that entered the Port Lligat house was censored; Gala would scissor out her face in a neat circle. Although her mental faculties were unimpaired, she had begun to lose her hearing as she neared her eighties. The boisterous gatherings that Dalí so much enjoyed left her bewildered and on the defensive. Her cynicism and her cruelty hid a hollowness that neither Dalí's companionship nor her young lovers could fill.

Meanwhile, Dalí's sexual fantasies became more pronounced. One female friend of the artist, who preferred to remain unidentified, once accompanied Dalí to a bullfight in Barcelona. 'Afterwards,' she said, 'Dalí insisted on going to a brothel. According to Dalí all Spanish men visited whorehouses after the *corrida*. So I went along. The girls paraded before us, but Dalí was interested in watching only. I think he liked having me along as security, so the other girls would keep a bit of distance.' If any prostitute tried to fondle Dalí, he would brush away their hands muttering, inexplicably, 'The stain, the stain.'

Aside from sex, Gala had another expensive vice – gambling. Her intuition with the fortune-telling cards, she believed, could also help her win at the roulette tables of Monte Carlo. The reverse was more often true. In the mid–1960s and early 1970s Gala reputedly squandered vast sums gambling on both sides of the Atlantic. One night in New York, where roulette is illegal,

Gala reportedly lost all the cash she had saved to pay their bill at the St Regis hotel. Determined to hide this loss from Dalí, she dispatched a confederate on the first Switzerland-bound flight to withdraw funds from her account. 'One reason why she liked being paid in cash for Dalí's work,' Sabater said, 'was that it allowed her complete liberty of action in her private life.' One benefit of travelling across the Atlantic by ocean liner instead of airliner, as Gala soon realised, was that she could play in the ship's casino for six days at a time.

Gala's insistence on being paid cash to hide her losses was recalled by Reynolds Morse, who paid $140,000 in a vast quantity of pesetas for a canvas, *The Ecumenical Council*. The Dalís were sailing from New York that day, and Gala began stuffing stacks of peseta notes inside her suitcase, her steamer's trunk – even inside her underwear – to smuggle the currency past customs officials. Her haughtiness frightened them off, and she was never caught.

'This gambling streak seemed to run against her character,' Sabater remarked. 'She was incredibly stingy. A five-dollar restaurant bill could put her in a foul mood, and yet she'd gamble away huge quantities.' Gala's willingness to sign a contract for Dalí's services often depended on how much she had lost the night before at the roulette wheel. The Dalís' ex-secretary claimed that Gala's obsession with gambling waned in the early seventies, though some former business partners maintain that Gala continued gambling heavily at Monte Carlo and that she even established a separate bank account for this purpose. 'Dalí never found out about Gala's losses,' Sabater maintained. Unfortunately, Gala's avarice led her into some deals that were artistically dubious and downright illegal. Despite their riches, Gala was convinced that their expenses – hers especially – were so colossal that they would soon be spending more than Dalí made. She drove Dalí remorselessly. Once she admitted to Eduardo Fornés, a Barcelona publisher, that she had been 'nasty' with the painter: 'She said she had a bad conscience because she sometimes locked Dalí into his studio without food and wouldn't let him out until he finished some long-overdue canvas.'

Dalí's artistic reputation will be judged by his oil paintings, over which he agonised, but most of the money poured in through the sale of prints, lithographs, postcards and fairly distasteful commercial ventures. Gala swiftly realised that every scrap of paper on which Dalí signed his name was worth something. Reynolds Morse once told Dalí he was cheapening himself by painting an advertisement for Pepto-Bismal, the liquid for stomach upsets. Dalí held up a cheque for $50,000 and said in his thick Catalan accent: 'Can you earn this much money in five minutes, Mor-r-rse?'

Dalí and Gala also cashed in on the popularity of lithographic prints. In theory, an editor would commission an original work from Dalí, a limited number of signed prints would be made from the original, and the plates from which the prints were made would then be destroyed. In practice, however, Gala would demand that the printer secretly run off more than the agreed-upon number of prints. So, if collectors were assured that they were buying one of 1250 'original' prints, they were in fact being cheated into buying one out of, say, 7000 prints. Such a large number of extra 'originals' on the market obviously reduced the value of the collector's print. A French art editor, Jean Schneder, claims that when he tried to persuade Dalí to stop mass-producing these signed works of art, Gala interceded and threatened to break off business unless Schneder complied with the fraud. It was not long after, in 1981, that Gala convinced Dalí to sign 35,000 blank sheets and, claimed the Spanish press, these sheets were then resold to several editors, who then put whatever image they wanted on the blank sheets and sold them as Dalí originals.

Respectable art dealers in New York, Paris and London had suspected that something was going on. For years, the print market had been swamped with second-rate Dalís. The more prestigious art galleries refused to touch anything by Dalí unless it was pre-war. As the reputable dealers stepped away, there were dozens of less scrupulous and unpleasant replacements.

Besieged by all the hustlers, Gala's suspicion of even her friends eventually bordered on the pathological. Reynolds and Eleanor Morse happened to visit Port Lligat when Dalí was doing a publicity stunt for Air India. Baby elephants were romping on the beach, with Dalí and a dozen Hindu girls in sparkling saris: Gala surveyed the spectacle with the loftiness of a maharani as the Morses approached. The two couples had not seen each other for several months, yet, instead of the warm welcome expected by the Morses, Gala reacted with hostility. 'You've just come to capitalise on the publicity, haven't you? Now get out of here!' she yelled.

The Morses needed no prodding. Dalí rang them in Barcelona to apologise for Gala's outrageous behaviour but the Morses were still angry. For two years they refused to see the Dalís. 'Then we had a tearful reunion, and all was forgiven,' said Morse in an interview.

One bizarre account of Gala's role in passing off Dalí fakes comes from Manuel Pujol Balades, a self-confessed art forger. One summer evening in the mid-seventies, Pujol hurried down the path to Port Lligat as the sun set. Gala had summoned him. The sheltered bay brimmed with shadow. French spear-fishermen were dragging their inflatable Zodiac rafts ashore. A few hippie campfires were already being lit inside a ring of tents on the sandy shore. A wisp of flute music floated over the water.

These were the pilgrims of Port Lligat. The sixties had brought Dalí back in style. The Rolling Stones sought entrance to his sanctuary, as did every hitchhiking hippie who found an LSD trip mirrored by the meticulous hallucinations of a Dalí work. A teenaged girl appeared once tattooed with a Dalí moustache. Dalí was amused by the new wave of adulation. A familiar complaint in the past had been that nobody astonished him; waiters did not bring him a telephone under a covered dish when he asked for a lobster. Now, outside his door in Port Lligat, there was a long queue of admirers willing to serve up his surrealistic surprises – lobsters, telephones or any other fantastic whim of his. In the afternoon, Dalí would allow the more spectacular specimens of youth and utter weirdness to congregate inside his garden, beside his phallus-shaped swimming pool. When Dalí tired of his marvellous court, Gala would usher them out and at the door would also relieve the guests of any drawing or signed souvenir that Dalí, in a joyful mood, might have given them.

Pujol had graduated from all that; his audience was private. He could make out the giant eggs on the stone wall surrounding the Dalís' olive trees, the two colossal statuary heads leaning against each other in repose or sorrow – it was impossible to tell which. Were they Dalí and Gala? In his leather jacket with long fringes on the sleeves Pujol looked like Buffalo Bill. To complete the image he had a small goatee and black, shoulder-length hair; he was in his mid-twenties.

Pujol had started forging as a teenager, turning out comic books so a Spanish publisher would not have to pay royalties to Walt Disney. Now he was being paid a lot of money – by Gala – to do 'Dalíesque' watercolours. It was better than Mickey Mouse, but the pay still wasn't enough. In the mid–1970s Dalí had developed the symptoms of Parkinson's Disease, and, although his shaking ceased as if by magic whenever he took up a brush, he was no longer inclined to churn out the watercolours and the fast prints. The money tap was drying up and Gala had an irrational, almost pathological, fear of poverty, even though her handbag was always filled with uncashed cheques that she hoarded long past their expiry date. One editor of Dalí prints, Pierre Argillet, who always tried to pay Gala in cash, recalled: 'Gala never took the money calmly – she would seize it. Then she would place it under her buttocks. She would sit on the banknotes for the half-hour or so that I was entitled to converse with her. Basically, Gala needed lots of liquid cash for her gigolos.'

Pujol the forger thought he deserved more for his labours. It bothered him that Gala paid by the hour ('just like a plumber's work') when he suspected that she turned around and sold his work as an original Dalí for ten times as much money as he received.

Pujol stepped by the wrecked hull of a fishing boat in which Dalí had planted a cypress which grew from its ribs like a tapered green flame. The door to Dalí's home was small and battered, just like those of the nearby fishing huts. Pujol was ushered inside by the maid and escorted past a stuffed grizzly bear that served as a coat-rack. He thought he knew the house well, but he found himself guided to an unfamiliar room. It was perfectly round, with a Turkish-style divan running in a full ring around it. A fire burned in the white hearth, its flames reflected in the crystal bust of an emperor. The most revered object in Gala's round room was not a Dalí painting but a Russian icon which had been in her possession for many years; it is possible that she could have brought it out of Russia when she left to marry Eluard. She would lock the door and pray before the icon, kneeling and touching her forehead on the ground.

With Pujol, however, Gala had less reverential thoughts in

mind. She sat beside the fire with Enrique Sabater, who had gradually replaced the stalwart Captain Peter Moore as the Dalís' private secretary. ('One day,' said Captain Moore, 'Gala said she'd found someone younger and better looking. She told me to clear, off.') Gala did not rise for Pujol but clasped his hands, allowed him to kiss her on both cheeks, then beckoned him to sit beside her. He brushed against Gala's tanned legs; she was wearing shorts. 'I couldn't help but think: What fine legs she has for an old woman,' Pujol said later in an interview.

'Sabater,' commanded Gala, 'bring us Perelada.'

The secretary re-emerged in the round room carrying a bottle of pink champagne and three glasses. At first they talked business. Gala explained how she thought Pujol was a good enough artist to be allowed the 'honour' of being selected to do work 'inspired by *el Maestro*'. Pujol would later have the pleasure of seeing one of his oil 'inspirations' sold by a London art auctioneer for many thousand pounds as an original Dalí. Another bottle of champagne was fetched, then another, and it dawned on Pujol that he was doing most of the drinking.

He tried guessing Gala's age. There were none of the scars or exaggerated stretch marks left by cosmetic surgery, yet the skin on her face seemed smooth and tight. Gala sneered at women who resorted to face-lifts; she relied on an entire suitcase loaded with unguents and expensive creams to keep herself looking young. She could have passed for late fifties, early sixties. She was in her late seventies.

When Gala complimented Pujol on his talent, his ego soared. 'Gala, who had recognised the genius of Dalí and Picasso, was telling me I was a real artist. It was heady stuff,' recalled Pujol. Gala even liked his new leather jacket. She was effervescent.

She had been sitting on the divan with her legs curled up under her like an excited little girl. Then, flirtatiously, she stretched them out across Pujol's lap and began rubbing her foot against the inside of his thigh. This was Gala's technique. Introduced to a desirable young man, Gala never wasted time in reaching across and stroking his genitals, with a fair amount of aggression. Sabater had disappeared, probably for more champagne.

'Please, don't,' said Pujol gently.

'Don't what?' Gala said, still massaging the inside of Pujol's thigh with her bare foot.

Pujol lifted away Gala's foot and said drunkenly: 'You have such nice legs that I'm starting to forget that you're old enough to be my grandmother. And I don't want to forget that.'

Gala jumped up. She was enraged. 'Pujol,' she hissed, 'you're a little swine.' Her voice was so chilly it seemed to Pujol that the room temperature had dropped 10 degrees. 'Sabater!' she called imperiously. 'Pujol likes champagne. Pink champagne. I want every bottle in the house. Bring them to the bathroom. We are going to give our rude little piggy a bath.'

Pujol was ordered to lie in the tub. Gala put in the plug and began to shower Pujol with champagne.

'Hey! My new jacket!' shouted Pujol. He was almost in tears, and too drunk to resist the humiliation. Bottle after bottle was emptied over him.

'You see, Pujol, if you act like a pig you are treated like one. Now lap it up! What's wrong? You said you liked champagne.'

Finally, Gala grew tired of her sport with Pujol and he was allowed to stagger away. The champagne had ruined his jacket.

'I had the worst hangover the next morning, as you can imagine, but I went back to apologise to Gala for what I had said. After all, she had offered me work.'

Gala refused to see Pujol. He returned to the house every day for several weeks before she finally relented and let him in. 'She needed me,' said Pujol.

Politically, in the 1970s, Gala and Dalí became captives of their own notoriety. Dalí had followed with rising fear the newspaper accounts of the John Paul Getty kidnapping in Italy. He was convinced that Mafia thugs were planning to grab him next, and if the gangsters did not get him then the new generation of Spanish revolutionaries certainly would. In 1975 Dalí's ultra-reactionary politics landed him in trouble again. As Spain was easing itself out of forty years of dictatorship, Dalí made the ill-timed remark that Generalissimo Franco should have executed more people. Anti-Francoists blew up Dalí's favourite chair at the Duran Hotel in Figueras. Soon the Dalís were receiving death threats, and Sabater began to carry a pistol. Sabater's many enemies accused him of terrorising Dalí to secure his total dependence on him. Dalí was easily frightened. Oriol Maspons, a photographer, was staying at Port Lligat with Dalí one evening when some hooligans hurled a few rocks at the house. 'Three stones, and Dalí fled that same evening in his Cadillac,' Maspons told me.

If the Dalís travelled anywhere, they began to insist on security precautions fitting for a Third World despot. Gala was not immune to this paranoia. Dalí's biographer, Secrest, recounts how the Dalís once tried to keep their departure from New York a secret – without success. When the pharmacist at the St Regis pleasantly told Gala he was sorry to hear the Dalís were leaving the hotel so soon, Gala, vexed, spat in his face.

It must have aggravated Gala's unease that Dalí now had two regular female companions, both glamorous. According to one acquaintance, Gala felt so insecure that she seriously feared Dalí wanted to get rid of her. This was pure fantasy; Dalí never allowed Gala's position to be threatened by any woman. One regular companion was Nanita Kalachnikov, an intelligent and aristocratic Spanish woman married to a Russian. Dalí called her 'Louis XIV' because her profile resembled the French king's. Kalachnikov had three daughters and never considered Dalí more than an enthralling friend. His other companion was Amanda Lear, a tall, blonde model-cum-singer whom Dalí claimed had once been a very pretty Vietnamese man. Dalí felt safe with Amanda Lear; he could enjoy the company of a young and stunning 'woman' without feeling any sexual threat. Lear has written an autobiography, *My Life with Dalí*, in which she insists that Gala, once her initial mistrust had been overcome, pleaded with her to marry and care for Dalí after she died. However, according to Sabater, relations between the two women were not so amicable: 'Most of the time, Dalí would only dare ask Amanda around – in New York, Paris or Port Lligat – when Gala was off on her excursions.' In a way, Gala may have been grateful to Amanda Lear and Nanita Kalachnikov for keeping Dalí out of her hair, but even during her long absences Gala kept in touch so that Dalí could never stray too far from her sphere. In fact, Gala's excursions were becoming more frequent. She had found a new companion; it was a perilous relationship – and it nearly caused her to sacrifice Dalí.

15

Exterminating Angels

In 1973, a musical, *Jesus Christ Superstar*, was causing a stir in New York. The title alone appealed to Dalí's flamboyant mysticism. He and Gala did not venture down to Broadway much; they were worried about being mugged. Instead, they requested the theatre to send round publicity photos of the cast. They were especially intrigued by the leading actor, Jeff Fenholt, who had long auburn hair and a Renaissance face of luminous pallor. The Dalís had a penchant for sizing up actors and inviting them to the hotel suite afterwards for closer inspection. If the actor proved as handsome without the greasepaint and bright costumes, Dalí, on Gala's behalf, would unabashedly ask him to remove his clothes with a view to posing for his next masterpiece. Vanity usually overcame their modesty and few actors or actresses refused the invitation.

Out of the blue Fenholt received a request to attend one of the Dalís' Paupers' Teas. He accepted, and it was an invitation that was to affect severely Fenholt's life for many years after. 'Gala was good for me and bad, too,' Fenholt told me over the telephone from California. 'She inspired me so much that I became destructive. I tried to shut the world out with booze and drugs.' After his strange relationship with Gala ended, Fenholt went from acting Christ on stage to being the lead singer in Black Sabbath, a satanic rock group.

Gala and Dalí were sitting at a long table in the King Cole cocktail lounge when Fenholt and some other actors from *Jesus Christ Superstar* came in. For the occasion, Gala had chosen a red dress with a chunky green-stone necklace. Immediately, as if in a trance, she rose to her feet – which she seldom did even for royalty – walked straight to Fenholt and took both of his hands in hers. 'Come,' she said. 'You sit by me.' Gala would not let go of Fenholt. Later, she confided triumphantly to a friend: 'I feel like his grandmother and his lover.'

There is no doubt that Gala was vain, but she believed that her attractiveness radiated from inside. She did not waste time on face-lifts or new wardrobes to captivate her young companions. She had her favourite 'costumes' which she wore year after year, and when they wore out, she would have identical copies made. She was an insecure dresser, counting on Dalí to provide an artistic dash to her ensemble.

Gala was smitten by young Fenholt. Her infatuation with the drug addict William Rotlein and even her devotion to Dalí were overshadowed by this new passion. Fenholt was possessed of a lean beauty, considerable talent and the addled conviction, forged by the adulation he received on stage acting Jesus Christ and the ingestion of many drugs, that he was a sort of messiah. In all seriousness, Fenholt told an interviewer from *Women's Wear Daily* that he was the 'source of God'.

The Dalís' secretary, Sabater, was once invited to Fenholt's home for the traditional American feast of Thanksgiving. 'At the end of dinner, Fenholt gave me a framed picture of Jesus Christ. Not on the cross or anything, just a portrait of a very beautiful Christ from the shoulders up. Then Fenholt tells me: "Here, take it, Enrique. This is me." I was stunned.'

Gala had the perfect retreat for herself and Fenholt. She had always wanted her own castle, preferably a good many miles from Dalí and the insistent blare of his circus. She had thought of Tuscany, perhaps. However, Dalí did not want Gala that far away from him, so he sent Sabater up in a plane to scout out castles in the region around Gerona that might be up for sale. The aerial photographs revealed a small medieval castle encircled by a tiny feudal village in the hills near La Bisbal. It had a high-walled garden with orange and plane trees, and roses climbing up the walls of a chapel. The rolling landscape of woods and fields even looked like Tuscany. In the early 1970s Gala set about decorating the yellow sandstone castle in her own style, austere and baronial.

Her retreat to Pubol castle happened at a time when she was preparing herself mentally for death, and needed to divorce herself from Dalí's pestering. While in New York, she and Dalí once a week would disappear from their retinue of jesters, sexual acrobats and millionaires and quietly pray together at a secluded altar in St Patrick's Cathedral. In Pubol, Gala's devotions were strictly private. Her bedroom was adorned with crucifixes and Russian icons. Once a week she would borrow the old key to the chapel from the village mayor, Benjami Artigas, close the massive oak door behind her and pray in dark solitude. She had no interest in attending mass or discussing her faith with the parish priest. There in the quiet chapel one wonders if the image of her Jesus Christ Superstar, sensual and yet ethereal, shone in her mind like a golden icon. It would fit with the impression one has of Gala as a woman who swung between extremes of carnality and spirituality with no repentance. Fenholt, for Gala, embodied these two extremes. The handsome actor was also a pleasant distraction from the accelerating collapse of her own health.

Her last-minute spirituality, it seems, was born not out of guilt or fear, but out of expectation; she wanted to clear her mind and could not do so with Dalí's many distractions. Death was not something that terrified Gala much. 'The day I die,' she said, 'will be the best day of my life.'

If Gala was trying to reach some peace within herself, the effort did not necessarily make her more forgiving. During the summer Gala divided her time between Pubol castle and Port Lligat, where she still harassed Dalí into painting harder. One summer in the mid–1970s Cécile arrived. She thought she could wear down her mother's animosity through sheer perseverance. Cécile rented a room in Cadaqués from Catalina Romans, a former maid of the Dalís who had opened up a hairdresser's salon. Catalina remembers Cécile, then in her fifties, as a thin, rather pathetic woman who, once a day for three months, undertook the tiring walk over the hill to Port Lligat to knock on the door of her mother's house. Gala never answered the door herself, and she ordered the servants not to admit Cécile. From her room over-looking the entrance, Gala would have watched her daughter's desperation grow every time she was turned away. Finally, Cécile could stand it no more and left Cadaqués.

At Pubol castle, Gala was even more selective of her guests, and enforced the rule that only Fenholt could be admitted without her written invitation. No exception was made for Dalí.

The Broadway musical closed not long after Fenholt and Gala first met, leaving 'Jesus Christ Superstar', as Gala persisted in calling him, free to travel between New York and Catalonia whenever the summons came. According to Sabater, Fenholt was terrified of flying alone, and Gala sometimes ordered her secretary to catch the next plane from Barcelona to Madrid, change there for New York, drive to Fenholt's home in New Jersey ('Jeff had the most beautiful wife and child,' recalled Sabater. 'I couldn't understand why he would leave them.'), head back to John F. Kennedy Airport with Fenholt and accompany him on the first flight back to Spain – all within twenty-four hours. 'It was exhausting,' said Sabater, 'but Gala wanted Jeff.' The invitation to Fenholt was always open, and Sabater had to deliver the actor straight from New Jersey to Pubol. 'There were some very spiritual things happening in Pubol castle,' Fenholt remarked vaguely. 'Strange vibes. Gala and I had this close bond. I guess you could say there was a definite pairing-off between us.'

Despite his avowed rediscovery of Catholicism, Dalí's religious practices remained idiosyncratic, at the very least. Fenholt once made the mistake of trying to get Dalí to kneel and pray with him. 'It happened about three weeks before his breakdown. I tried to get him to pray with me. But Dalí became violently mad and ordered me out, shouting. It was the only time that Dalí ever lost his temper with me.'

Gala was obsessive about cleanliness but disorganised. One night, when jet-lag kept Fenholt from sleeping, he began rummaging around for reading material. 'There was a stack of old magazines, *Playboy* and things like that, in one of the back rooms. Maybe it was a closet. Mixed in with all this I found a manila envelope, so I opened it, right? Inside there were signed prints that Dalí had done back in 1936. They were worth a lot of money. Gala didn't believe me until I showed them to her,' Fenholt reported. 'What surprised me was that the prints were old but the envelope was new. It wouldn't surprise me if someone were trying to rip them off.'

After *Jesus Christ Superstar* finished its Broadway run, Fenholt decided to devote himself full-time to a singing career. Gala helped. She filled Pubol with guitars, a piano and the most advanced electronic music equipment. Fenholt often brought with him tapes of songs he had written and played them to Gala before anyone else had heard them. As she had done with Eluard and Dalí, Gala succeeded in convincing Fenholt that she was art's ultimate arbiter. It seems she had both the gift for inspiration and the power to bend creative and insecure men to her will.

Fenholt also held Gala under his own influence. Quite simply, Gala loved him more than he desired her, and to some in the Dalís' circle it seemed that Fenholt enjoyed manipulating the elderly woman's infatuation for his own profit. Once he complained to Gala that he could not visit her in Pubol because his luggage, with many belongings, had been destroyed in a fire. Gala gave Fenholt nearly $20,000 to replace the lost items. Another time Gala approached Morse, who was in Europe with the Dalís, and begged him to take $38,000 in cash to Fenholt in New York; without the money, Gala told him, Fenholt would die. Morse, who did not want to be mixed up in illegal currency smuggling, brushed off Gala's request: 'Well, let him die, then.'

Sometimes the emotional games turned rough. Since Dalí could not be coaxed into an aeroplane, he and Gala crossed the Atlantic by ocean liner. On one occasion Fenholt had promised Gala that he would wave her off at the pier, but he was nowhere to be found. The whistle blew, and Gala was frantic. 'She was very distraught,' recalled Sabater. 'Gala was pacing around the deck shouting "Jeff! Jeff!" But he never came. I think he liked stringing her along so that she would want him more.' Fenholt's excuse was that the police would not let him on the pier because his hair was too long. Gala of course forgave him, but she spent the entire sea voyage wondering why Fenholt had not turned up. Was he angry with her? Had he lost interest? Had he been run over?

Gala always forgave Fenholt, even when she suffered. One evening, at the St Regis in the late 1970s, Sabater was roused from his bed at 2 am by a knock at the door. Sabater opened it to find Gala standing there with blood streaming from her shin. The wound was nasty; Sabater could see jagged bone, and he called down for an ambulance.

'What happened?' asked Sabater. He knew that Gala had been at Fenholt's apartment on 54th Street. 'Where's Jeff?'

Gala shrugged.

'I was angry with him for not taking care of Gala,' recalled Sabater. 'So I called Fenholt's place. There was no answer.'

'How did you get here?' Sabater asked Gala.

'By myself, by taxi,' she replied tersely. It was a terrible injury for anyone to have, especially a woman in her eighties, and

Sabater was amazed that Gala had the strength to find her way down the stairs from Fenholt's apartment, flag down a taxi on the streets of New York and limp along to his room for help.

Medical assistance finally arrived. Sabater kept dialling Fenholt's number. He even telephoned a house that Gala had bought for Fenholt on Long Island, but no one answered. For ten days Fenholt disappeared. After insisting as much as he dared, Sabater finally extracted from Gala a version of what had happened that night, though he did not believe it: 'Gala claimed that she just hit her shin on the sharp end of a cocktail table, but I have my doubts. The wound was so deep. And, if it were only an accident, why did Fenholt run off?'

Fenholt failed to respond to over twenty telephone messages that I left on his answering machine and with his Arizona agent in my attempt to contact him for his explanation of the story. In any event, Gala's ardour for Fenholt was not cooled by this episode. As well as the Long Island house, valued at $1.25 million, Gala also gave him several Dalí canvases.

Gala was convinced that Fenholt would become famous, and she grew frustrated at his failure to make any mark in the music business. The overblown orchestral rock music with which Fenholt had gained his fame was blasted out of fashion by punk rock. A pretty face and a good voice no longer impressed record producers, who were searching for a raw and primitive sound like that of the Sex Pistols. Gala championed Fenholt with the same zealousness – and failure – she had exhibited during the early 1930s trying to hawk Dalí's absurd inventions in Paris. It reached the point when Gala, in her evangelical efforts to promote Fenholt, grew blind to the artistry of others, even Dalí. She once mocked Dalí with the meaningless insult that he was 'no good because he could not play the guitar as well as Jeff.'

When Dalí's companion, Amanda Lear, began to attract attention on the European disco circuit, Gala could not contain her envy. She telephoned Amanda Lear in Greece to reproach her. 'I find this success of yours most extraordinary,' Gala said caustically. 'You sing so badly! I listened to your record again last night and you sound like an old drunk. When I think of Jeff's talent I find your success quite incomprehensible. But of course you're so cunning. . . . You are always talking about Dalí: Dalí this, Dalí that. After all, people are only interested in you because of Dalí.'

Gala was also abnormally jealous of Fenholt's wife. She once told a woman friend of Dalí's: 'Do you know what that bitch has done? She's pregnant again, that's what. Poor Jeff, doesn't she know the burden that she's placing on him?'

With Gala's past lovers, Dalí may indeed have channelled the fury of jealousy into his art – or so he claims – but Fenholt was a threat. Gala's obsession with the young singer began gnawing into her devotion to Dalí. This had never happened before. Deprived of her constant care, Dalí felt as if his oxygen supply had been severed at a time when he most needed it. His health had begun faltering from 1975 onwards. His cowardice and obstinacy made it impossible for anyone but Gala to handle him. The sicker he became, the more irrational were the demands he made on Gala. She complained of being unable to leave his bedside, even for a visit to the hairdresser's. Gala felt trapped; Dalí had drained her energy and drawn her away from Fenholt, who was spending more time in America drugged and dodging her telephone calls. It was all turning horribly spiteful. Gala and Dalí bullied and physically assaulted one another. They, who had surrounded themselves with young and beautiful people, could not bear the sight of each other's decrepitude, nor their own. Worst of all, Dalí was too terrified of his illness to fight it, and nothing Gala could do, either through gentle pleading or by blows from her tiny fists, could shake Dalí from this terror. In Paris, according to Amanda Lear, Dalí fell to the pavement in a spell of madness and refused to get up while Gala beat him with his cane and cursed him as he writhed under her blows. Dalí's vanity also prohibited him from seeing close friends. He told Amanda Lear over the telephone: 'I want you to remember me as I used to be. You must never suffer the disappointment you would feel if you saw me now. Never. I could not stand it.'

An account similar to this sad pavement scene came from Dalí's studio assistant, Bea, who told me: 'By the late 1970s, the Maestro's attacks were becoming more frequent. He and Gala were fighting a lot. Sometimes in the middle of it all, Dalí's rage would unhinge him and he'd collapse on the floor, squirming about for a minute or so. Gala would act abusively towards him, trying to force him to react to her.' Bea added: 'Strange, though, even with his illness, as soon as Dalí grabbed a brush, his hand steadied.'

In February 1980 Gala and Dalí both caught flu and seldom left their room at the St Regis. Their illness darkened their perceptions of New York; it was colder and meaner than they had remembered. They complained of poor service at the St Regis and refused to eat the hotel food. They had come to suspect and envy the fortune of their secretary, Sabater, as the Dalís did of anyone who profited from them.

Paloma Chamorro, a Spanish television jounalist who conducted one of the last interviews with Dalí while Gala was still alive, reported:

Sabater had hundreds of millions of pesetas in his bank account, while Dalí had maybe 20 million. What gave Gala and Dalí so much pleasure was knowing that they could command this man who was so much richer than them to act as slave. Dalí would say: 'Sabater, I'm going to take my siesta now. I want you - not somebody else, you – to wake me up at 4 o'clock. And I want a glass of orange juice squeezed by your very hands. And I want you to find two transvestites and have them walking through the door the instant you serve the orange juice.'

Sabater had been a football player, travel agent and photo-journalist before he earned Dalí's approval by taking a photo-graph of the artist staring down at a fly on his moustache. Sabater was a fast learner; he could pilot a small aircraft, shoot a pistol, fix hotel bookings and negotiate lucrative deals for the Dalís and, of course, for himself. It was worth squeezing the orange juice.

During that long, final winter in New York, Gala leaned heavily on Mia Rentjens, a Dutch ex-model who read tarot cards. Because of her ability with the cards, Mia became Gala's confidante, prob-ably the only female friend that Gala ever had, but, again, there was a mean twist to this relationship, according to Sabater. 'Mia was mad about Dalí. She worshipped him. And Gala would love tantalising Mia by bringing her into the room next to Dalí but refusing to let her see him. Gala and Dalí would laugh about it afterwards.' Mia denied this: 'I got to see Dalí as much as I wanted. He even let me hold his cane sometimes.' Once Gala was assured that Mia had no intention of profiting from their friendship, she opened up, showing Mia little secrets like the ring with a love note hidden inside, written in Russian.

Gala would fetch Mia from the hotel lounge. 'Come,' Gala said. 'We've got to work.' Mia accompanied Gala upstairs and the two women sat on Gala's bed, as Mia read the Oracle of Belline, tarot cards designed by a French clairvoyant. Gala consulted the tarot on her own once a day, using ordinary Spanish playing cards, but she trusted Mia's spiritual talents. 'Gala was smart in the mediumistic sense. She could tell what people were after,' Mia told me. 'But she made some surprising mistakes in judgement.' According to Mia's account:

> Gala would often be tired. I could see the strain on her face. 'Keep it simple,' she'd say. And we'd just dive into it. The sessions would last for two hours and she was always delightful.
>
> Sometimes Gala would jump off the bed and go running out like an excited little child to check on Dalí. She was always very protective of him.

Gala took Mia's interpretations of the tarot seriously. One reading, in particular, confirmed what Gala had already suspected: a betrayal. 'I got the Cat in connection with Fate and Lust,' said Mia. 'This meant treachery over negotiations.' Immediately Gala's suspicions fell on Sabater. He was banished from his ceremonial place at the end of the St Regis banquet table, and his seat was bequeathed to Mia. 'You and Jesus Christ Superstar are my only friends,' Gala confided.

Death never surfaced in their long talks. 'She never brought up the subject,' Mia recalled, 'but I remember asking her if she was going out for a stroll. Gala replied, in French: "*Je ne me promène jamais. Je marche.*" ("I don't stroll. I stride.") I think that was her attitude about a lot of things, maybe even death.'

That February 1980, Dalí's health never seemed to recover. Under advice from Morse and Michael Stout, their New York lawyer, the Dalís flew back to Spain. Dalí was eventually persuaded to check into the Puigvert clinic in Barcelona. Gala wanted to fly back to New York; she had faith in American medical technology and, besides, she yearned for Fenholt. Reynolds and Eleanor met Gala leaving the Barcelona clinic on a day when the news had been bad. A team of doctors and psychiatrists concluded that the chances of Dalí ever regaining his health and sanity were small indeed. The blow to Gala was all the more brutal because she had deluded herself into believing, as she told one newsman, that Dalí was 'indestructible as a rock'. Dalí, however, had always prayed that he would die before Gala, even though she was ten years older.

The Morses offered Gala their sympathy and help, but Gala at first rebuffed them. She may have been spiritually ready for Dali's death, but not to witness the mental and physical decay of his genius. Then Gala broke down, hugged Reynolds Morse and cried for comfort.

16

The Last Cadillac Ride

In 1929, during Gala and Dalí's first encounter, as they scaled the cliffs that rose sharply above the sea near Cape Creus, Gala had pleaded with Dalí to kill her, to hurl her tiny body into the blue emptiness. In a sense, Dalí may have finally carried out that request, over half a century later.

However, death was not quite how Gala had envisaged it.

In February 1981 the Dalí entourage decamped from Cadaqués to the Alfonso XIII suite at the Hotel Meurice in Paris. Late one evening Enrique Sabater was awoken by the painter hammering frantically at the door connecting his suite with Dalí's. 'Sabater, help!' shouted Dalí. Sabater by then was fed up with catering to the Dalís' outlandish whims and had thought of resigning. Since Gala suspected him of treachery after the tarot reading in New York, she had told the desk at the Hotel Meurice to keep a note of his telephone calls and expenses. This time, though, Sabater could not ignore Dalí's urgent, panicked pleas. Dalí forced the lock and burst into Sabater's room.

Barefoot, Sabater accompanied Dalí back into the artist's suite. Gala lay on the floor beside her bed. She was in great pain and glowering at Dalí. Her silence was venomous. As Sabater lifted her on to the bed, she winced.

He called the Meurice desk, which over the years had grown accustomed to strange events in the Dalí suite. (Once the artist's pet ocelot had escaped and sprinted to the top floor, terrorising the other guests, until one of the doormen, an ex-boxer, grabbed the animal by the tail.) Sabater demanded that the hotel doctor be roused. Gala was obviously badly injured. Dalí stood behind Sabater, anxiously looking at Gala but afraid to move any closer to her.

'What happened?' Sabater asked Dalí while they waited for the doctor. Incoherently, Dalí began mumbling that the two had been lying in their separate beds and somehow she had rolled off on to the floor.

Dalí's excuse was too muddled to make any sense to Sabater, whose thoughts were concentrated on how this accident could be concealed from the press. The accidental tumble – if that was what had genuinely occurred – was serious. Gala was a fragile eighty-six-year-old.

The doctor diagnosed two broken ribs and lesions along her leg and arm. An ambulance was called, and Gala was rushed to the American hospital in Neuilly. By then it was dawn. Again, Sabater asked Dalí what had really happened. Gala's side, arms and legs were blackened as if by blows and Dalí had a bruised eye. This time Dalí told the truth. He had struck Gala with his cane, again and again, and she had punched him back.

There were many reasons for the fight, and Sabater had his own suspicions, as he told me in an interview: 'Gala needed enormous quantities of money. Dalí was too sick to produce anything – he had been for a while. Gala had literally forced Dalí to put his fingerprint on a document that, as Dalí found out, signed away some reproduction rights Dalí didn't even own. Trembling, Dalí said: "Sabater, please, please help me against her." I almost wept.'

Dalí had also received news that Gala had lavished gifts of cash and several of his own paintings – worth over a million dollars – on Jeff Fenholt. The musician had auctioned off his collection of Dalí canvases at Christie's in New York. The auction was the first that Dalí had heard about Gala's presents to Fenholt, and this provoked a terrible fight between the couple. Until then, Dalí had been impressed with Gala's power to woo the young and handsome Fenholt; he did not know what it was costing him.

Gala had become so besotted with the actor that, according to some press reports, she actually threatened to leave Dalí on the grounds of his impotence, a rather tardy complaint after half a century together. In any event, there is no doubt that Gala had little patience for the weary task of attending to the caprices of her invalid husband. In her last interview, Gala remarked: 'Being loved matters little to me. Personally, I don't love anyone. . . . As for my relations with Dalí, they are what they are. We don't have these ordinary types of problems; we live in freedom [from each other] despite everything. We are not a couple.' For Dalí, who had relied on Gala's mothering, on her lioness's protection and zealousness, her change in attitude was the ultimate betrayal.

Sabater moved swiftly to stop the newspapers from getting a whiff of the Dalís' brawl. He issued a press release sticking to Dalí's original story that Gala had tumbled out of her bed. Then he bought Dalí a pair of dark glasses to hide his black eye. Gala may have kept her silence at the beginning, but her resentment of Dalí continued to burn long after she checked out of the American hospital. Back in the Hotel Meurice, she showed her bandaged arm to a waiter bringing up room service. 'See this?' she said haughtily to him. 'Dalí did this to me.' 'And she pushed me under the bed,' retorted Dalí, who was also in the room. Before this, Gala and Dalí had always been careful to preserve the illusion of being a contented couple, at least in public.

Gala pined for Fenholt. In her dotage, 'Jesus Christ Superstar' had become a symbol of almost divine carnality. She wanted to rejoin him in New York but she was too weak and deaf to travel alone. There were no willing escorts for the journey – not even Sabater, who on 12 March announced he was leaving. The toil of caring for the Dalís twelve to fourteen hours a day for more than nine years may have earned Sabater plenty of money, but it had also wrecked his marriage. What clinched it for him was Gala's decision to go behind his back and sign illegal contracts with Jean-Claude du Barry. The head of a 'modelling' agency, du Barry had been chief procurer of boys and girls for Dalí's voyeuristic fantasies and male companions for Gala. Du Barry once bragged to Secrest, the Dalí biographer, that his service to Dalí was similar to that of the offical taster in Louis XIV's court, only du Barry was Dalí's 'officier des queues', which translates as 'officer of the rear ends'. According to Sabater, Dalí distrusted du Barry so much that whenever he visited Port Lligat Dalí ordered the servants to prevent theft by locking the doors and windows.

When Sabater handed in his resignation, Gala spat in his face. However much they may have disparaged Sabater and mistrusted him, they had grown dependent on him and his departure was a shock. Not only had Dalí and Gala lost each other, but their loyal servant had also deserted them. They were old and sick and could not care for themselves. Dalí's outspoken support of Franco had also earned him the enmity of many in the new democratic Spain, and they were not even entirely safe in Paris, where communists picketed the Hotel Meurice.

Reynolds Morse and the Dalís' New York lawyer, Michael Stout, rallied to their aid. A replacement had to be found for Sabater, swiftly, to stem the spreading influence of du Barry. The best candidate was Robert Descharnes, a French photographer, who had collaborated with Dalí on several film and book projects. 'It's up to you, Robert,' Morse told him. The only drawback to Descharnes was that Gala detested him. According to Sabater, Descharnes would be forced to leave at mealtimes because Gala found him so offensive that she refused to sit at the same table with him. Later, after Gala's death, Descharnes stopped Morse and many of Dalí's old friends from seeing the invalid painter, claiming he was only following Dalí's orders, that *él Maestro's* vanity forbade him from showing friends how he had deteriorated so rapidly. However, Dalí's old friends accused Descharnes of isolating Dalí to increase his power – and profit – over the ailing artist.

One of Descharnes's first jobs was to arrange a private flight for the Dalís back to Port Lligat, via Perpignan. The Hotel Meurice suite was costing $4000 a week, and for months the Dalís had neglected to pay their servants at Port Lligat. It was to be the final trip for Gala and Dalí.

Even more worrying than Dalí's financial condition was his health. For years Gala had plied him with pills from a large medicine case with which she always travelled. No one knew what exactly she carried in the case, but Gala's treatment of her own many illnesses had given her a reasonable knowledge of drugs. Friends say, however, that as Gala slipped into senility her pharmaceutical skills began to fail. The pills got mixed up; Gala forgot which medicament worked for what; and, worst of all, the chemicals she fed Dalí often reacted dangerously with the treatment prescribed by specialists. Morse was convinced that the symptoms of Parkinson's Disease exhibited by Dalí could have been caused by Gala's toxic mixtures. Dalí may have bickered endlessly with Gala, but she was still the only person capable of persuading him of anything. Her word was supreme: several months earlier, she had stopped nurses in a clinic from carrying out the treatment ordered by medical specialists. When

Dalí was bothersome, she would feed him tranquillisers, and she used pills to rouse him.

Sometimes Gala's insults turned the normally timid Dalí apoplectic with rage. His cane no longer served as a stage-prop but as a weapon, and he constantly lashed out at the servants, at his assistant, Isidoro Bea, and at Gala. His vengeance burned through in his art; the title chosen for his new canvas was *Exterminating Angels*.

However, Gala was not to be cowed. In an investigative book into the artist's final days, called *El Ultimo*, the writers claim that when King Juan Carlos paid a visit to the couple in Port Lligat in August 1981 Gala tried to persuade Dalí not to wear his red fishing cap. 'How can I not wear it?' replied Dalí, yanking the cap off. 'Am I supposed to show the king the wound that you've opened in my skull with your shoe?' Gala would also bully Dalí over money, if the term 'bully' can be applied to a diminutive, eighty-six-year-old woman. Mark Rogerson, author of an investigation into the Dalí forgeries entitled *The Dalí Scandal*, claims that once, when Dalí was slow in rising from bed to sign a contract, Gala began punching him, 'She was wearing rings and they cut Dalí's face,' writes Rogerson. 'Stout said: "Gala, why did you hit Dalí with your hand with all the rings on?" She replied: "Because I wanted him to know he had been hit." '

The sparring was constant, pathetic in its pettiness and debilitating not only for Gala and Dalí but also for anyone unfortunate enough to be at Port Lligat. Any pretence at civility was dropped; it was as though the approach of death impelled them to unburden the rancour piled up for half a century. Gala's sole escape – to Pubol castle – was blocked. She was too ill, and hiring nurses for both her and Dalí was considered an unnecessary extravagance.

The unremitting violence between the two led to rumours that the accident which caused Gala's death – a broken femur – may have been Dalí's fault, a push down the staircase. It was not quite as dramatic as Dalí had originally intended in 1929, when he contemplated pushing her off a cliff; but for a quavering old woman a few stairs would have been just as treacherous. I have no way of proving this, but I believe that Dalí was unbalanced enough by his illness and rage to have wanted to cause Gala serious harm. The official version, however, is that on February 24, 1982 Gala slipped while climbing out of the bath and her fragile thighbone chipped like china. Gala was rushed to the Platon clinic in Barcelona, but there was nothing the doctors could do. It was as if all parts of her tough little body blew out their seams at once. Her lucidity faded to a dim flicker; hallucinations and ghosts preyed on her. Perhaps there were images of Cécile as a young girl, abandoned with fever in a Cadaqués hotel room while Gala entered Dalí's planetary otherness, never to turn back. Her arteries were too worn to withstand the transfusion needles. Her skin, which she had treated with every kind of rejuvenating elixir, erupted in dozens of hideous sores.

Although Gala was ten years older than Dalí, nobody – especially not Dalí – thought that she would die first. When Gala was in the Barcelona clinic, Dalí simply did not want to hear about her failing health. His sole occupation at the time was reading scientific journals. Dalí's cousin, Serraclara, also said that the artist was obsessed with his 'auto-aesthetics', in other words, his drooping features. It was harder for Dalí to ignore Gala, though, when the medical specialists brought her home to die in Port Lligat. Her sickbed was set up next to his.

On 26 May 1982 Dalí's aides decided, inexplicably, to camouflage Gala's impending death. A press release was issued stating that Gala was 'fine and at this very moment up out of bed'. It was a shocking lie. At Pubol, workers were ordered to speed up construction of Gala's crypt, a structure of black brick placed in a cavernous hall where the serfs had once paid homage to their feudal lord. Dalí wanted his crypt next to Gala's, connected by a window so the two corpses could be neighbourly after death. The crypt was guarded by the statue of a large black horse, a prop from a portrait Dalí had done of Generalissimo Franco's daughter. Two weeks before the rosy press release, it had seemed that Gala would die any moment. Dalí summoned Joaquim Goy, the priest of Pubol, to perform the last rites.

The priest was driven across the Ampurdan plain to Port Lligat by Benjami Artigas, the round-bellied mayor of Pubol and butcher who, according to one newspaper account, had planned to profit from Gala's stay in the village castle by selling a Dalí brand of sausages. Artigas also had bad news for Dalí: the crypt was nowhere near finished. In addition, the mayor was afraid that the Catalan government might raise official obstacles to the castle burial. This enraged Dalí. 'If I can't bury her in Pubol, I'll bury her in Monaco or in New York,' he shouted at Artigas.

The maids at Port Lligat had prepared Gala for the priest's visit. Her hair was impeccably brushed, and she had been dressed in a white blouse of brocaded silk. Crucifixes and rosaries hung everywhere. The priest found Gala immobile, with a lost and vacant gaze in her eyes. Dalí kept vigil beside her, and as the priest made the sign of the cross and administered extreme unction, Dalí automatically began to mumble a paternoster.

Artigas took advantage of the many doctors and visitors bustling in and out of the room to peek at Gala. According to him, 'She looked absolutely finished.' The priest, who had more experience of the dying than Artigas the butcher, thought otherwise, and on the return drive to Pubol he confided to Artigas: 'This one's going to take her time.'

In Port Lligat, Dalí wandered around the house, asking his lawyer, Miguel Domenech, his cousin, Serraclara, Antonio Pixtot, an artist and family friend from Cadaqués, and all the others if they thought Gala would die. Considering that Gala had just received last rites, the answer was so obvious that nobody softened the truth.

Gala, however, tenaciously hung on to life far longer than her doctors thought possible. The priest had given her extreme unction in April, but Gala clung on until June, dipping in and out of a coma. The length of her illness had blunted much of the shock of her death; Dalí began to look on Gala as little more than a nuisance, a tiresome ghost. Serraclara said: 'At the end, Gala died abandoned in a corner.'

Several days before her death, a visitor came to see Gala. It was her daughter, Cécile. Somehow the secret that Gala was dying had reached Cécile in France. In all probability, someone in the Dalí entourage had assumed that a mother would naturally want to be reunited one last time with the daughter she had brought into existence. Cécile was told that time was short. She hurried from France to Port Lligat and went straight to the Dalí house. A servant answered the door and told Cécile to wait. It is not known whether her arrival coincided with one of Gala's few lucid moments, or whether Dalí himself made the decision, but when the servant returned, it was to tell Cécile that Gala, even on her deathbed, refused to see her daughter. It was the final humiliating rejection for Cécile, who visibly staggered away from the house. She did not attend Gala's burial.

Gala's bed had been positioned next to a window facing east towards Cape Creus. That had always been Gala's view: dawn's first rays striking the dark blue bend of the cape. She had sailed to that place with a strong fisherman, had swum in its deep currents, tossed her head back and opened herself to that fisherman on his tiny wooden boat in the undulating sea. There had been many summers, with many different men. It was there that she had sealed her strange pact with Dalí; through this pact, Gala had gained a freedom both spiritual and carnal. It enabled her to become monstrous, yet pure.

Dalí had asked for a folding screen to be placed between his bed and hers. Gala gasped like a drowning swimmer and her frail body was already cadaverously still. In this state Gala frightened Dalí. 'She won't let me sleep,' he complained.

On 12 June, just as the sunbeams spurred over the side of Cape Creus and lit the room, Dalí rose creakily from his bed. Painting had bred in him the habit of waking early, even though he was no longer capable of executing more than a few trembling doodles. Dalí edged aside the screen that separated his bed from his wife's. It is said that Gala's head lay on the pillow facing Dalí. Her eyes, 'eyes that could pierce walls', were wide open, but Gala was dead.

With Gala dead, I can at last, as writer, intrude into the narrative. While researching this book, I imagined Gala's character as being like a set of painted Russian dolls, with one fitting inside the hollow of the other, and that by the time I had worked my way down to the last doll I would have discovered an explanation – or an excuse – for Gala's wickedness.

There was no excuse. At times, as I was writing the book, I had moments when I envied Buñuel for trying to strangle Gala. She had no talent of her own; she was bad-tempered, obnoxious and coarse. She drove Dalí too hard and shook him like a money tree. Had Gala been less greedy and more loving, Dalí would undoubtedly have produced greater art. For all her mystical intuition, she invariably ended up trusting thieves.

Yet she was the key to deciphering Dalí's work; Dalí says as much. She gave him the sexual understanding that enabled him to dominate his own demons. I do not know whether Gala accomplished this feat simply by tolerating Dalí's fear of female genitalia or, as some friends suggest, by diverting his attentions to her other orifices. It does not matter; what does is that, as he explains in *The Unspeakable Confessions of Salvador Dalí*: 'Gala allowed me to accede to the spiritual delights of Eros, she knocked out the barriers of my childhood fancies, my death anxieties. She cured me of my self-destructive rage by offering herself as holocaust on the altar of my rage to live. I did not go mad, because she took over my madness.'

It would be wrong to suggest that Dalí's masturbatory frenzies drove Gala to seek other partners. The pattern of her debauchery was set long before she met Dalí; Eluard may have nudged her into affairs, but Gala did not need encouragement. She was sexually voracious and amoral. Even in her eighties, Gala was cheating on her young lover.

Gala's amorality had many roots. In childhood she learned to rise above the shame of her mother's relationship with the rich 'stepfather', which was sinful by the orthodox standards of Russian society. She defied her siblings' revolt against her step-father and ingratiated herself with him. Surrealism, which substituted a delirious anarchy for the corrupt values which had led to the Great War, provided Gala with an ideological flag for her libertinage. As a provincial little Russian girl eager to prove herself with the Parisian literati, she willingly participated in the sexual experimentations of Eluard, who was nearly as voyeuristic as Dalí.

With Dalí, Gala gained a sexual and monetary freedom that few women throughout history have enjoyed. As long as Gala looked after him and fed him, acted as go-between with reality and clawed off predators, Dalí sanctioned her affairs; his own sexual proclivities were so bizarre that he could not do otherwise.

Gala knew the rules of civilised behaviour; she simply chose to ignore them. In a sense, I admire her independence and the vigour with which she flouted moral standards. She was also wonderfully egalitarian in her tantrums: she would insult French cabinet ministers and waiters alike.

Her sadism was unforgivable. She lacerated both strangers and loved ones. She treated her first husband, her daughter and her Russian family miserably. She humiliated and spurned Cécile, in particular, beyond any justification. Gala's only pretext was that caring for Dalí was so consuming she had no room in her life for anyone else. This is indefensible nonsense: Dalí was the chief victim of her sadism. She did not care for Dalí; she dominated him. At the Marbella clinic, when Gala shooed away a nurse who tried to give medication to the ailing artist, she did so not because she mistrusted the doctor's prescriptions but because she did not want to relinquish any of her power over Dalí. His enslavement to Gala was such that when she died he could not survive for long without her.

Arturo, the chauffeur, was one of the first to reach the room after Gala's death was discovered. He later told journalists: 'When madam died, el señor had the same reaction as always. He said she wasn't dead, that the madam would never die.'

There was no time to waste. Spanish law forbids any corpse to be moved until a judge has seen it. The justice system also rarely allows private burials outside cemetery walls. Gala had insisted on being interred at Pubol. Monarchist that he was, Dalí also wanted to be buried inside his castle, and the magistrates had reluctantly agreed to make an exception for el Maestro and his wife. After all, the king had given him the title of the Marquis of Pubol. However, it was decided by Dalí's entourage that to dodge any legal complications, Gala's corpse was to be driven secretly to Pubol. Then they would officially announce that she had died there.

To carry out this surrealist – and highly illegal – charade of moving the body, they stripped Gala naked, wrapped her in a rough blanket and stretched her out on the rear seat of the midnight-blue Cadillac. A nurse was to ride along so that, if the speeding Cadillac were stopped, it would seem as though Gala had died *en route* to hospital. The ever-faithful Arturo agreed to drive. Arturo was a good, smooth driver but he could not prevent the corpse from slamming against the doors with a thud every time the car twisted down the mountain road to the Rosas plain.

The mayor, Artigas, had been called and was waiting in the dirt courtyard outside the castle gate when the Cadillac drove up. 'I couldn't help thinking,' said Artigas, 'how small Gala was when she was alive. The times she would ride by in that big car,

I could never see her head, just her black bow. I wondered whether she would still be wearing that bow, even now she was dead.'

Artigas closed the gate behind the Cadillac and watched as Arturo lifted the body out. It was now noon, and hot. The dogs of Pubol barked as the car pulled up. The air was scented with trellis roses and oranges from the castle garden, mixed with manure and straw from the village barns. The corpse weighed less than 100 pounds, but it was not an easy burden for Arturo, strong though he was. Gala had befriended Arturo when he was a young fisherman. He had taught her Catalan when they sailed out to set the lobster nets, and he had taken her body into his arms many times before.

Arturo carried Gala upstairs to her bare, white room, decorated only with a few Russian icons hanging by the door. Gala was slid between the sheets of her bed to create the impression that she had died in her sleep at Pubol. Artigas telephoned the mortician from nearby La Bisbal, and then Arturo returned to fetch Dalí from Port Lligat.

In the meantime Dalí had telephoned King Juan Carlos in Madrid to break the news. An official statement to the effect that Gala 'had died surrounded by the constant attention of Salvador Dalí' was drafted and read to several newspaper editors, who hurriedly sent cameramen to Pubol castle. There was much morbid curiosity. Dalí, after all, had vowed to cannibalise Gala. 'For me,' he often remarked, 'eating Gala would be the deepest expression of love.'

Dalí, however, had lost all appetite for publicity. Originally he had wanted no funeral ceremony, only to be alone with Gala a last time before the priest entombed her. Dalí, however, was too shaken for such an intensely personal act. On arrival at Pubol, he went straight upstairs without viewing Gala's body, which the mortician had placed in a glass-topped coffin. Gala's body was dressed in a favourite suit of red velvet and wore rings, designed by Dalí, which, as Artigas noted with some awe, were 'nearly as large as her hands'. The mortician had rouged her olive cheeks and attached the black Chanel bow to her hair. The ceremony was intimate: the servants, Dalí, Domenech, Descharnes, Serraclara, Pixtot, the three doctors who had attended Gala, Montserrat Dalí, a favourite cousin of the painter's, and her companion, José Gudiols, an art historian and collector. Dalí, for all his rediscovered mysticism, was impatient with the religious aspects of the funeral and turned down a suggestion by Serraclara to have Gregorian chants sung as the coffin was lowered into the black crypt.

The burial service was in Catalan, but even the sonorous echo of his own language through the castle failed to lure Dalí downstairs. Finally, two hours after Gala's body was placed inside its tomb, Dalí gathered enough courage to visit the crypt. It was to be his final resting place too.

Leaning on Serraclara, his cousin, Dalí entered the crypt. The ancient room had four stone arches. The horse and the two giant giraffe heads that Dalí had wanted were in place. It seemed that Dalí drew strength from the sight of his own art; his step steadied, and he placed a single flower on Gala's black tomb.

Then, said Serraclara, 'Dalí waved me away. He wanted to be alone with Gala. Dalí kneeled – not because he wanted to pray. Dalí knew nothing of that.' After a brief moment, Dalí rose and said bravely to Serraclara: 'See, I don't cry.' But the tears were flowing down his face.

After Gala's death, Dalí lost his will to paint or even live. He shut himself up in her room, pulled the curtains and refused to let any sustenance or friends relieve his darkness. He forbade anyone from mentioning Gala's name. Alone, in the tower of his surrealist museum, he raged against his decrepitude, terrified of his approaching death.

Bibliography

Books

Ades, Dawn, *Dalí*, Thames & Hudson, London, 1982
Buñuel, Luis, *My Last Breath*, Jonathan Cape, London, 1984
Cowles, Fleur, *The Case of Salvador Dalí*, Heinemann, London, 1959
Dalí, Ana Maria, *Salvador Dalí visto por su hermana*, Ediciones del Cotal, Barcelona, 1949
Dalí, Salvador, *The Secret Life of Salvador Dalí*, Vision, London, 1949
Dalí, Salvador, *The Unspeakable Confessions of Salvador Dalí*, W. H. Allen, London, 1976
Dalí, Salvador, *Diary of a Genius*, Hutchinson, London, 1966
El Pais, *El ultimo Dalí*, Ediciones El Pais, Madrid, 1985.
Eluard, Paul, *Lettres a Gala (1924–1948)*, Gallimard, Paris, 1984
Eluard, Paul, *Lettres de jeunesse*, Seghers, Paris, 1962
Ernst, Jimmy, *A Not So Still Life*, St Martin's/Merek, New York, 1984
Ernst, Max, *Ecritures*, NRF, Paris, 1970
Gateau, J. C., *Eluard et la peinture surréaliste*, Droz, Paris, 1980
Gershman, Herbert, *Bibliography of Surrealist Revolution in France*, publisher unknown, 1969
Gibson, Ian, *Federico García Lorca*, Ediciones Grijalbo, Barcelona, 1985
Goëmans, Camille, *Goëmans: Œuvre, 1922–1957*, publisher unknown, Brussels, 1970
Guardiola Rovira, Ramón, *Dalí y su Museo*, Editora Empordanesa, Figueras, 1984
Hugnet, George, *Pleins et déliés*, Authier, Paris, 1972
Jean, Marcel, *Histoire de la peinture surréaliste*, Seuil, Paris, 1959

Jean, Raymond, *Eluard*, Seuil, Paris, 1968

Lear, Amanda, *My Life with Dalí*, Virgin, London, 1985

Levy, Julien, *Memoirs of an Art Gallery*, Putnam, New York, 1977

Mann, Thomas, *The Magic Mountain*, Penguin, London, 1960

Melly, George, *Swans Reflecting Elephants*, publisher and date unknown

Morse, Reynolds, *Salvador Dali: A Panorama of his Art*, Salvador Dalí Museum, Cleveland, 1974

Nadeau, Maurice, *Documents surréalistes*, Gallimard, Paris, 1968

Orwell, George, *Homage to Catalonia*, Martin Secker & Warburg, London, 1938

Penrose, Antony, *The Lives of Lee Miller*, Thames & Hudson, London, 1985

Rafael, Santos Torroella, *Salvador Dalí Corresponsal de J. V. Foix 1932–1936*, Editorial Mediterrania, Barcelona, 1987

Rogerson, Mark, *The Dalí Scandal*, Gollancz, London, 1988

Romero, Luis, *Todo Dalí en un rostro*, Blume, Barcelona, 1975

Sadoul, Georges, *Souvenirs d'un témoin*, publisher and date unknown

Sanchez Vidal, Agustin, *Buñuel, Lorca, Dalí: el enigma sin fin*, Editoriales Planeta, Madrid, 1988

Santos Torroella, Rafael, *Salvador Dalí, corresponsal de J. V. Foix, 1932–1936*, Editorial Mediterrania, Barcelona, 1986

Santos Torroella, Rafael, *Salvador Dalí escribe a Federico García Lorca*, Poesia (Min. de Cultura) nos. 27–8, Madrid, date unknown

Secrest, Meryle, *Salvador Dalí*, Weidenfeld & Nicolson, London, 1986

Thirion, André, *Révolutionnaires sans révolution*, Lafont, Paris, 1972

Tual, Denise, *Le Temps dévore*, Fayard, Paris, 1980

Valette, Robert D., *Livre d'identité*, Tchou, Paris, 1967

Vieuille, Chantal, *Gala*, Favre, Lausanne, 1988

Waldberg, Patrick, *Surrealism*, Thames & Hudson, London, 1965

Periodicals

Blanco y negro, Cécile Eluard, Madrid, 20 April 1988

Europe, Paris, 1962

La Gaceta Literaria, Madrid, 15 May 1931

Littérature, Paris, 1919–24

The New Yorker, 1945, 1947
Plein Marge, 'Soirées chez Gala', Henri Pastoureau, Paris, December 1986
La Révolution Surréaliste, Paris, 1924–9
Revue de l'Art, Flammarion, Paris, 1971
Le Surréalisme au service de la révolution, Paris, 1930–3

Interviews

Albaretto, Mara, art collector, telephone interview, summer 1988
Argillet, Pierre, art editor and collector, in Barcelona, spring 1988
Bea, Isidoro, Dalí's assistant, in Barcelona, summer 1988
Bergery, Bettina, friend of the Dalís, in Paris, autumn 1986
Bowles, Paul, writer and composer, in Tangier, summer 1988
Buñuel, José Luis, film maker, telephone interview, winter 1987
Dalí, Montserrat, the painter's cousin, autumn 1984
Eluard, Cécile, Gala's daughter, in Paris, 1984
Faucigny-Lucinge, Prince de, art collector, in Paris, autumn 1987
Fenholt, Jeff, singer and actor, telephone interview, winter 1987
Fornes, Eduardo, art publisher, in Barcelona, summer 1987 to spring 1988
Kalachnikov, Nanita, friend of Dalí, in Marbella, spring 1987
Jaroljmec, Lidia, Gala's sister, in Vienna, autumn 1986
Lear, Amanda, singer and TV personality, in London, spring 1985
Morse, Reynolds and Eleanor, art collectors, in Barcelona, autumn 1987
Pujol Balades, Manuel, artist, in Barcelona, autumn 1985
Rentjens, Mia, tarot card reader, telephone interview, winter 1987
Romans, Catalina, former maid of the Dalís, in Cadaqués, summer 1987
Sabater, Enrique, the Dalís' former private secretary, on the Costa Brava, in Barcelona and Madrid, summer 1987 to spring 1988
Santos Toroella, Rafael, art critic, in Barcelona, spring 1988
Sauguet, Henri, composer, in Paris, autumn 1986
Serraclara, Gonzalo, Dalí's cousin, in Barcelona, autumn 1986
Stout, Michael, Dalí's lawyer, telephone interview, spring 1988
Tual, Denise, film maker and writer, in Paris, 1986

Index

CHILD STAR

AN AUTOBIOGRAPHY

SHIRLEY TEMPLE BLACK

'An extraordinary piece of work' *Daily Mail*

For the first time, Shirley Temple Black – the quintessential child star of the 30s and 40s – tells in her own words the extraordinary story of her life as an actress.

Starting her career at the tender age of three, she was soon performing alongside such stars as Gary Cooper, Cary Grant, Ginger Rogers and (her favourite) Bill 'Bojangles' Robinson. However, all was not always sugar-sweet aboard the Good Ship Lollipop: she was made to perform in exploitative movies by unscrupulous studio bosses; there were numerous kidnap threats and even a murder attempt against her; she made a disastrous teenage marriage to an incorrigible womaniser. Eventually, though, she found lasting love and happiness with ex-naval officer Charles Black, and waved goodbye to Hollywood for ever. Filled with revelations and personal anecdotes, CHILD STAR is at once candid, funny and poignant – and an inspiration to all.

'An awesome book, far richer than the average Hollywood apologia' *Sunday Times*

'Temple tells it like it was, with great good humour, more charity than is frequently warranted and healthy dollops of cynicism' *The Times*

NON-FICTION/AUTOBIOGRAPHY   0 7472 3303 9   £4.99

R I C H A R D
BRANSON

THE INSIDE STORY

MICK BROWN

"An excellent biography – engaging but far from idolatory" *Guardian*

ADVENTURE CAPITALIST

Unorthodox entrepreneur and City businessman, philanthropist and intrepid transatlantic yachtsman and balloonist: not yet forty, Richard Branson is all these and more. How did he achieve so much so quickly? What is the key to his success?

In his bestselling biography, Mick Brown examines Branson's life and analyses his highly idiosyncratic business techniques in dissecting the many elements that make up 'the Branson phenomenon'.

"Well researched and attractively written" *Observer*

"An important biography" *Daily Telegraph*

"That rarest of all things, a biography which meets its own claims to be both authorised and critical" *Sunday Times*

"Mick Brown has a good ear for choice anecdotes and an entertaining way of passing them on" *Guardian*

NON-FICTION/BIOGRAPHY   0 7472 3469 8   £4.99

More Autobiography from Headline:

Patrick Macnee

BLIND IN ONE EAR
AUTOBIOGRAPHY OF AN AVENGER
'Amusing and often painfully honest' *Daily Express*

The bowler hat. The rolled umbrella.
The bespoke suit. Patrick Macnee is known
to millions for his portrayal of that epitome of
the English gentleman, John Steed, in the
internationally successful television series *The
Avengers*. Born of aristocratic parents, he went
to prep school and Eton. But the conventions of
upper-class English life end there. Pa was a
drunkard and a gambler; Mama was a lesbian,
who moved in with her formidable lover Evelyn,
bringing her bemused, be-kilted son with her.
Expelled from Eton for running the school
'book', Patrick made his first tentative steps into
the footlights. The limelight took a little longer;
he did not achieve overnight cult status as
John Steed until he was nearly forty. The rest,
as they say, is history . . .

Witty, inventive, bizarre and eccentric, *Blind in
One Ear* is the extraordinary autobiography of
an extraordinary man.

'Rich in anecdotes . . . but what sets aside this
book is the quality of Patrick Macnee's writing
about his crazy childhood.'
Mail on Sunday

NON-FICTION/AUTOBIOGRAPHY   0 7472 3305 5   £3.99

PETER GABRIEL

AN AUTHORISED BIOGRAPHY

SPENCER BRIGHT

'Well-researched and intelligent' *Today*

Born of a gentleman farmer father and a doting musical mother, he had a conventional middle-class upbringing.

At public school he was a quiet and conscientious pupil.

Then he discovered rock 'n' roll.

While still a schoolboy of seventeen, Peter Gabriel founded the band that was eventually to become the seminal group of the seventies, Genesis. When he left in 1975, speculation was intense as to what he would do next. Few would have predicted that, despite long periods of silence, he would join that elite handful of rock superstars who command both the respect of the critics and the adulation of fans worldwide.

Flamboyant on stage, shy and serious in real life, Peter Gabriel rarely gives interviews and so has remained something of an enigma. Now the man himself, his friends and colleagues have decided to give Spencer Bright their full cooperation for this book. The result is a sympathetic and provocative biography which at last reveals the man behind that legendary mask.

'Welcome and enjoyable . . . the first serious attempt to understand one of the few genuinely original talents residing uncomfortably in the wacky world of rock 'n' roll' *Venue*

'A compelling biography' *Daily Mirror*

'A compelling read' *Record Mirror*

NON-FICTION/BIOGRAPHY   0 7472 3231 8   £4.99

A selection of bestsellers from Headline

FICTION

THE DIETER	Susan Sussman	£3.99 ☐
TIES OF BLOOD	Gillian Slovo	£4.99 ☐
THE MILLIONAIRE	Philip Boast	£4.50 ☐
BACK TO THE FUTURE III	Craig Shaw Gardner	£2.99 ☐
DARKNESS COMES	Dean R Koontz	£3.99 ☐

NON-FICTION

THE WHITELAW MEMOIRS	William Whitelaw	£4.99 ☐
THE CHINESE SECRET SERVICE	Faligot & Kauffer Translated by Christine Donougher	£5.99 ☐

SCIENCE FICTION AND FANTASY

MAD MOON OF DREAMS	Brian Lumley	£3.50 ☐
BRIDE OF THE SLIME MONSTER Cineverse Cycle Book 2	Craig Shaw Gardner	£3.50 ☐
THE WILD SEA Bard III	Keith Taylor	£3.50 ☐

All Headline books are available at your local bookshop or newsagent, or can be ordered direct from the publisher. Just tick the titles you want and fill in the form below. Prices and availability subject to change without notice.

Headline Book Publishing PLC, Cash Sales Department, PO Box 11, Falmouth, Cornwall TR10 9EN, England.

Please enclose a cheque or postal order to the value of the cover price and allow the following for postage and packing:
UK: 80p for the first book and 20p for each additional book ordered up to a maximum charge of £2.00
BFPO: 80p for the first book and 20p for each additional book
OVERSEAS & EIRE: £1.50 for the first book, £1.00 for the second book and 30p for each subsequent book.

Name ....

Address ....

....

....